# STRONG MARRIAGES, SECRET QUESTIONS

Every married person struggles. Everyone asks questions. And that's okay, says author Elizabeth Cody Newenhuyse. You can be happily, permanently married and still have things you wonder about. Things you don't want to admit to just anybody.

The questions may be secret, but they need answers. Especially in strong marriages meant to last a lifetime.

Newenhuyse has talked with scores of married couples about their joys and hurts, hopes and concerns. These conversations have convinced her of two things: it is normal to have secret questions, and strong marriages can grow even stronger. *Strong Marriages, Secret Questions* is her delightful blend of reality and optimism.

**Elizabeth Cody Newenhuyse** is senior editor of *Marriage Partnership* magazine. A frequent contributor to *Today's Christian Woman*, she has also written extensively for a variety of other publications including the *Christian Century*. Married since 1978, she and her husband, Fritz, live in Wheaton, Illinois, with their daughter, Amanda.

To Fritz

# Strong Marriages Secret Questions

Elizabeth Cody Newenhuyse

Published by
**Lion Publishing Corporation**
1705 Hubbard Avenue, Batavia, Illinois 60510, USA
ISBN 0 7459 1812 3

First edition 1990

**Library of Congress Cataloging in Publication Data**
Newenhuyse, Elizabeth Cody.
Strong marriages, secret questions / Elizabeth Cody Newenhuyse.—
1st ed.
ISBN 0-7459-1812-3
1. Marriage–United States. I. Title.
HQ734.N53 1990
306.81'0973—dc20                                    90-36244

Printed and bound in the United States

# Contents

# Acknowledgments

All books, but especially first books, have a lot of people standing behind them who deserve recognition and thanks. First, my deepest gratitude to my patient and wise editor, LaVonne Neff. Her touch is throughout this book; for that it is a better work.

And Harold Myra—master teacher, challenging mentor, firm friend. Always, Harold has been an unstinting encourager. Truly, this book bears his imprint.

Scott Bolinder first showed me that marriage was something rich and complex and worthy of exploring deeply and with imagination. He, too, has been a staunch friend and astute critic.

I am grateful to Christianity Today, Inc., for opportunities to learn and grow professionally. Thanks, too, to my colleagues Ron Lee, Harold Smith and Gregg Lewis—fine writers, exacting editors, and men of vision and journalistic integrity.

Gary Gnidovic not only designed the book jacket, he kindly listened to and perceptively counseled a first-time author going through the vicissitudes of the creative process.

A very special thanks to Walter Wangerin, Jr., for his generous sharing of wisdom and time.

Charlene Baumbich, Diane Eble, Barb Frost, O'Ann Steere and Virginia Vagt helped in various ways, from feeding my family to proofreading, typing, helping with ideas, and simply being there and being friends. The family at my church lent consistent prayer support.

My parents were and are my best cheerleaders—and, at least as significant, they taught me the importance of lively asking. This book, in a very real way, carries their stamp too.

My daughter, Amanda, has deepened my life and marriage far beyond anything I can here describe. She is a gift.

Finally, my husband. Fritz read the scrawled first drafts, offered incisive comment, helped brainstorm concepts. He also kept the world at bay while I was working. Mostly, though, he is the first reason I believe marriage is the better way. This book is for him above all.

# Author's Note

For this book I interviewed dozens of men and women, nearly all of them husbands and wives in their thirties and early forties, from various parts of the country. Some I interviewed together; more often I talked with them separately. I asked questions; they asked questions. Together we explored some answers—or at least learned what the right questions are.

This book would not exist without them. These men and women were candid, vulnerable, and generous with their time and hospitality. In nearly every case, except for a few names the reader may recognize, I have changed names and most other identifying details save number of years married.

My deepest thanks to all who shared their marriages with me—with the hope that others, too, may benefit from their stories.

Elizabeth Cody Newenhuyse
Wheaton, Illinois

# Chapter One
# Is This As Good As It Gets?

*After ecstasy, the laundry.*

Anon

The Mayfair Regent Hotel is tucked away on the most expensive one-block piece of real estate in Chicago. Pollution-hardy trees line the narrow street; graceful, humanely scaled buildings of marble and granite hint at rooms rich and mellow: worn leather chairs, brass library lamps, working fireplaces. The Mayfair is small, vaguely continental, definitely expensive. The Mayfair is where my husband and I celebrated—maybe "passed" is a better word—our tenth anniversary.

Obligations, like humidity, had been pressing in on all sides. Books to be written. Rooms to be wallpapered. Too many bills, not enough money. We lived with an unspoken sense of "child first, chores second, and us—whenever we can fit us in."

We sat on the floral upholstery in the tiny hotel room and stared at each other. Well, we're here. Isn't this fun?

Us. Whenever.

9

You can always tell the married couple. They're the ones not talking in the restaurant.

*Is this as good as it gets?* Yes. And no.

Most of the books make it sound so easy. If only couples learn ten ways to communicate, have a weekly "date night" and cut up those credit cards, their marriages—in the unfortunate parlance of the women's magazines—will enjoy new zip, zing and zest. I used to skim those articles and wonder why they rang so false. This isn't me, I thought. What's wrong with my marriage?

I've since learned, in twelve years of marriage, in editing a magazine on marriage, in reading true books on marriage—and, especially—in talking to real men and women, that *nothing* is wrong with my marriage. Not fundamentally. My marriage is, however, more complicated than the zip-zing-and-zest crowd would recognize. So are those other marriages I have been privileged to catch a glimpse of—more complicated, more delicately woven, more aching with beauty. And nastily cruel and miserably small-minded. And often bewildering, and perhaps boring more often than not. Sometimes all in the same day.

Why is marriage so hard? Why do so many once-soaring unions crash and burn? Why is infidelity so rampant? Why do so many marital relationships seem, well, *dutiful?*

### What's Another Word for Marriage?

I am an editor of *Marriage Partnership* magazine, and it's great work. We dissect, explore, celebrate and laugh about the married state. We try to give men and women help with their relationships. But we have this one unsolvable, persistent problem: the word *marriage* itself. One research expert advised us, "Stay away from the 'm-word' if you can. It's intrinsically boring." *Husband, wife, couple* aren't much better. Once I asked a friend, "What do you think of when you hear the term *married couple?*" "Bland!" she promptly replied.

Honesty test: How many of us—including those who, like me, believe that lifelong union between man and woman is God-ordained—still agree secretly with the following statements?

◆ Dating and courtship are more exciting, more romantic, than marriage.

◆ Monogamy may be wonderful, but it isn't necessarily workable.

◆ Married people tend to be overweight, complacent, dulled to each other.

◆ Other things—work well done, our children, the sight of stars, fascinating new friends—tend to evoke more passion than marriage.

Most of us, in at least some moods and seasons, would agree with some of these assertions. Yet most of us also would agree that boredom is not sufficient warrant for putting asunder what God hath joined together. The statistics are clear: married people live longer, have greater immunity to sickness, better mental health. Marriage usually produces children, who do better in an intact, thriving family than in a broken home. Marriage, simply put, is the better portion—the preferable way.

### The Riddle at the Heart
The paradox, then, is this: Man and woman were created by God to find each other and to live together for a lifetime; yet marriage is one of the most difficult enterprises we will ever undertake.

We often don't like paradoxes. Riddles may anger us. Yet, as I talked with couples about their

11

marriages, I increasingly became convinced that frustration besets us because we refuse to accept the paradox implied in the title of this book: *Every marriage is at times plagued by doubts, questions, secret struggles, feelings of "there must be more to life than this."* Some of those struggles have to do with the realities of the marriage bond, and as such they do not have a "solution." We live with them. Other questions do have hopeful, realistic answers.

In this book, I tell my own story, as well as those of dozens of other men and women. Some couples spoke to me together; more preferred to be interviewed separately. The majority have been married ten to twenty years. Because these husbands and wives spoke to me with candor and vulnerability, I have changed their names and other identifying details—but they are real. You might see yourself in some of their stories. Perhaps a few of their questions will sound familiar.

### Is That All There Is?

Hope and expectancy, the sense of possibility and promise, the refusal to accept what *is* for what *could be:* these things characterize we who stand outside the door to middle age. "We were the first to go to college in many of our families," says a forty-year-old husband. "Our parents gave us the feeling that the world was wide open, just waiting for us—not only in monetary terms but in achievement, too."

*There must be more!* That expectation has extended to our marriages. Some of the concerns wives and husbands shared with me would have been dismissed by previous generations as frivolous or simply would not have been understood. Before World War II, couples did not necessarily expect their marriages to fulfill, amuse or satisfy. Marriage was what you did to improve your economic station, to produce children, to meet community expectations. If you were happy in marriage, fine; but marital satisfaction was perceived more as a lucky accident than a life goal. Difficulties were met with the stoic fortitude typified by an older woman I once interviewed. The mother of ten, she came of age during the Depression and weathered incredible economic hardships while—and because—her husband was pursuing a vocational dream. "It must have been hard for you," I said. "No," she said briskly. "You do what you have to do."

No one says that anymore. We say, Why can't this change? How can we solve this? What about my needs? What about me—and my marriage?

Many of us have thought exhaustively about what we want out of life: fulfilling, remunerative work; bright, contented children; rich, engaging friendship; a renovated Victorian home furnished in the English cottage style; an abiding marital union that never bores and always reaches mutual orgasm. While we're at it, we'd like to help reforest Amazonia and brainstorm solutions to America's crack problem.

## Longevity Is Not Enough

So we're not willing to give up our dreams to settle for meaningless work and mediocre relationships. We look at our marriages of ten, fifteen, twenty years and, while we smile at their longevity in an era of broken promises, we also think that *longevity* is not enough.

Neither do the couples whose stories I tell. Many shared pain, wistfulness, disappointment, and a moving, gritty determination to stick to their commitment. Still others had come up with creative, even amusing solutions to the persistent irritations that plague all marriages.

I did come away from some of the interviews surprised by the couples' separateness. "Basically, we have very different interests," one husband told me. Another man said, "We're happy in our noncommunication." Yet both these men continue to hope for change.

## Separating the Siamese Twins

These and other conversations convinced me that there is a crucial distinction to be made between couples whose strength lies in their "twoness"— what David and Vera Mace, the founders of the American marriage-enrichment movement, have identified as the "companionship marriage"—and couples who have come to terms with, and even thrive on, the distances between them. Further, even those couples whose marriage is grounded in friendship and compatibility need to be separated at the hip.

An adage speaks of not looking at each other, but of looking outward together in the same direction. Much marriage counsel does exactly the opposite. Such advice sees marriage as existing in a vacuum. We're told to spend whole weekends with our "partners" (an unfortunately ambiguous term), discovering each other, touching, sending "I-messages." If we cannot give up entire weekends (as most of us cannot), experts advise us to set aside an hour each night to get reacquainted with one another. All solid advice—if a little shopworn. However, too often such guidance merely highlights the problems and increases dissatisfaction.

I know. I've been there; I've read the articles and the books and thought, "We don't do this. We don't hold periodic meetings assessing the state of the union. We don't have a lot of lists. We wing it. Yet I think we're reasonably happy. Aren't we?"

The truth is, many of the difficulties couples face have little to do with the state of the marriage and everything to do with the unavoidable external junk life throws at us. "I-messages" may help a couple weather a period of unemployment, but they don't make the pain go away. The pleasure of touch is lovely, but when one of us is staying up night after night to work through the latest budget reports or wait for a wandering teenager, the pleasure of touch lies asleep upstairs.

In the same way, marriages that are languishing in the dry periods that come to all relationships may find unexpected greenness and renewal from forces outside the union: a new friend, an appointment to the church's missions board, a shared home-renovation project. Those of us who are particularly sensitive to meteorological influences may find even a change in the weather bracing: I endured the hot, dry summer of 1988 in apocalyptic misery ("This is it—eco-death! Summer's changing forever!") and didn't much like anyone during those months. August, however, brought a sudden cooling, and my marriage and everything else looked as bright as the sharp blue days.

This, above all, is a book of reassurance. Everyone struggles. Everyone asks questions. The couples I talked with told about the junk life has thrown at them—and about the bracing effect of fresh external winds on their marriages. They were realistic, and often very funny, about the things that can't be changed. And they offered some pointers about things that *can* change.

Is this as good as it gets? Yes. And no. But maybe, for many of us, "this" is better than we realize.

# Chapter Two
# Is There More to Life Than the Daily Grind?

*If it wasn't for our to-do list, we*
*couldn't keep track of all the things we*
*don't get done.*

A wife in the trenches

Julie and Hank Weston were young, poor graduate students. They had two babies in diapers and were squeezed into a mobile home. Neither had time to do housework, so they let dirty dishes pile up and washed them on weekends. The system worked for them—until one day when old friends phoned. "We're passing through town and thought we'd stop by!"

Julie and Hank flew around, clearing away the clutter as best they could. But there was absolutely no place to put the towering mass of unwashed dishes. Finally Julie had an idea: "Let's put them in the bathroom!" She hid the unsavory load just in time.

When their friends arrived, the wife asked politely, "May I use your bathroom?"

Fortunately, the trailer had two bathrooms. Unfortunately, the bathroom that didn't have dishes had dirty diapers soaking in the tub. The Westons looked at each other...

## Time-Poor, Obligation-Rich

"Barely controlled chaos," says Atlanta marriage counselor Maxine Rock, is a "familiar pattern of family life in the tenth to fifteenth years of marriage." Couples with children, jobs, pets, houses, yards and bills are time-poor and obligation-rich.

We're running out of time, or we think we are. The phenomenon of time-hungry Americans has been amply caricatured: harried two-career couples with one hand on the microwave button and the other on the fax machine. More subtle, and possibly more insidious, is the feeling that our marriages are desiccating into mere enterprise—Marriage, Inc., the family business where we share a bed, a name, and the responsibility for finding a new floating ball for the toilet tank.

One by-product of the time crunch is the need to make the most of "together time." Unfortunately, together time too often is little more than a review of obligations: "We have to..." "Did you remember to..." "Where's the..." The result: our conversations take on either a sharp edge or a matter-of-fact flatness. Hardly the stuff of passion.

The slow erosion the daily grind can work on marriage has something to do with this. And where passion remains green, Marriage, Inc., brings other frustrations. Mason Harrell knows them all too well: "I don't think a week goes by that one of us doesn't say to the other, 'Life is too complicated.' But it's not the big issues—buying a home, deciding what school to send your kids to. It's the daily rat race."

Mason and Mary Lee Harrell have been married eighteen years. Both are easygoing Southerners who recently moved to New Orleans after a number of years in the Midwest. Mason, who has achieved some repute as a graphic designer, works in a home studio. Mary Lee has an earth-mother aspect to her; even though she spends much of her time shepherding five children from house to car to obligation and back again, she appears calm and unhurried.

The night before I talked to Mason, the Harrells had brought out some family photos, hoping to arrange them on the living-room wall in anticipation of overnight guests arriving in a few days. "We've been here over a year and haven't even hung our pictures," said Mason. "And that's what I *do* for a living." At 9 p.m. they spread out the photos to decide which to hang. Then, said Mason, "we realized it would take two hours to do this. Mary Lee went to bed. I put the photos back in the box. Then I sat and watched the news and Johnny Carson. The wall was still bare. Mary Lee was frustrated. I was frustrated."

The Harrells' photos remain in the box, a symbol of Mason and Mary Lee's struggle against the monster to-do list. Nearly every couple has at least one such undone task that symbolizes futility and chaos. For me, it's the refrigerator with its alien life forms biding their time in the cold darkness. For my husband it's the rotting bathroom windowsill. For Jim Donovan, a salesman in his early thirties, it's the Fiberglas insulation waiting in his garage. "I bought it three years ago, when we first moved into this house," he said. "It's been sitting out there all this time. I've never gotten around to installing it. Now I'm going to have to throw half of it out because it's gotten ruined with dampness."

Jim would ruefully identify with the image of the dull married couple. He and his wife, Cathy, a part-time secretary, have two preschool-age children. Jim travels frequently; Cathy still tries to keep a clean house. Both are involved, affectionate parents. What gets squeezed out of the schedule? Jim tells it this way: "We have a friend who's been on this kick of practicing the rhythm method for contraception recently: cycles of intercourse alternating with cycles of abstinence. I told him, 'We don't need to *practice* abstinence—we already abstain whether we want to or not!'"

## Partners in Frustration

Life used to be less difficult, we fondly imagine—at least where getting the chores done is concerned. "She takes care of everything inside the curb, I take care of everything else," said businessman John Koss, founder of the giant audio company that bears his name. Koss and his wife, Nancy, are typical of many couples who reared their families in the fifties and early sixties, when everyone knew who did what.

But most couples' reality is far different. While some couples make enough money to buy services, many more echo Mason Harrell's plaint: "We don't have time to do it ourselves, we don't know how even if we did have the time, and we don't have the money to hire someone who does know how."

The April 1972 premier issue of *Ms.* magazine featured a humorous article by Jane O'Reilly called "I Want a Wife." The phrase has gained currency among working women: "I have to pick up the dry cleaning. Nothing's defrosted for dinner. The dog needs heartworm medicine. I need a wife!" One couple I know has concluded that they also need a husband: they have posted a "husband list" on their refrigerator of jobs they hope to hire out.

Is anyone home these days? Is anyone working behind the scenes to keep everyone organized, fed, happy and in good repair? Yes—but in a growing number of cases the wife has been joined by the husband.

Sometimes, as Jim Donovan points out, such sharing can mean tiresome and elaborate negotiating: I did the dishes, so you read little Joshua a story. You did the grocery shopping, which is more fun, so now you have to fold laundry, which is unfun. "Everything has to be decided every time, it seems," says Jim. "It's as if we're constantly setting precedents." But Jim is *there*—scrubbing the kitchen floor at eleven the night before company comes, shooing children away as he hammers a tool shed together—and Cathy's not alone in the chaos.

Another couple, Ted and Dianne Nystrom, have developed the "principle of convenience" to divide up chores and child care. In other words, whoever can do the job most easily, does. If Dianne is in the kitchen and the garbage is overflowing, she takes it out. If Ted has to go to the store anyway, he'll drop their son at soccer practice. Dianne will mow the lawn. Ted will tuck the kids into bed. And, although Ted is in senior management at a Fortune 250 company and Dianne is an at-home mother, there is no "inside the curb/outside the curb" for the Nystroms—they share the work equally. One night, as Ted was preparing to leave the office for a hectic evening including daughter's concert, son's practice and men's choir rehearsal, his secretary said admiringly, "You're a good man, Ted!" "I'm a *tired* man," Ted replied as he galloped down the stairs.

21

Sharing the work does not mean approaching chores identically, however. Martha Howard-Davies, whose job requires her to take frequent trips out of the country, divides the load with Rob, her husband of twenty-two years. But they don't agree on everything.

"I've got this wonderful husband who keeps my life in order. But we go at organization, the daily grind, differently. When I'm in town, I cook; when I'm away, he cooks—using these really detailed meal plans."

Arguments about chores are nearly universal in marriage. Often—as with the Harrells' photos or the Donovans' insulation—couples stumble over one seemingly tiny thing. For Fran Meyers, it's socks. "Scott and I clean because we have to; not on any schedule. He would never notice a chore that needs to be done, and I'm just slightly less bad.

"It's not just that there's a clash over getting things done. When one isn't cooperated with on these things, one feels unloved. When he picks up his socks, I feel loved. If he leaves them all over the floor, they look like dead black fish, leering up at me in contempt. I finally had to *cry* to get my message across." The Meyerses used to fight about chores every Saturday, until they devised what Fran calls the "No-Nag Notebook," in which each of them writes down chores to be done. Result: the work gets done—without the nagging. (Except where socks are concerned.)

Many couples fall into what Jim Donovan calls the "who's-more-overworked" syndrome. The scenario is familiar: Husband (let's say) comes home, mind still buzzing from a difficult meeting at work. Wife greets him with, "Can you play with the kids for a while? I'm wiped out."

22

"*You're* wiped out?" he responds. "Do you know what I did today?"

"Ha!" comes the retort. "At least you got out."

## The Suicide Hour
Here's a fantasy. Mom, Dad and children all return from their respective pursuits around 5:30 in the afternoon and enjoy a fond reunion. The house is tidy, the breakfast dishes put away. There are no bills in the mail, only invitations and letters from old friends. The radio is tuned to soothing classical music. Mom and Dad enjoy a quiet time of re-entry while the children sprawl on the rug with their stamp collection. In the oven, bread is baking itself.

Here's the reality: "We don't cope. We scream at the kids. Sometimes Dale comes home and I'm sort of plastered to the couch, which is the signal for him to take over. Unless there's an 'important' ball game on TV. That makes it worse." Judy Hammond, married eight years and the mother of three children under six, works occasionally as a freelance writer. Her husband, Dale, is a high-school teacher and coach. Judy doesn't clean unless company is coming ("Why pick up if it's just going to get trashed again?"); Dale is, to a degree, what humorist Dave Barry would call "cleaning impaired."

Judy, a bright, thoughtful woman with a master's degree, feels keenly the stress of living with young children. Their house is small. Dale spends many weekends away with the team. Somehow, all the frustration converges on the Suicide Hour—that time between five and six when parents return from work, hungry and tired, and children greet them, hungry and tired (or, if the children are teenagers, do not greet them and probably are not even home).

Once again the dull ache of the home routine starts to thud in the brain.

"Never meet without an affectionate welcome," advises one counselor. Fran Meyers would agree. Fran and Scott have been married seventeen years. For fourteen of those years they each went off to their respective occupations, Fran as a personnel officer for an oil company and Scott as a civil engineer. Then their daughter, Meghan, was born and Fran decided not to return to her job. "We struggle with the re-entry period," she told me. "We talked about it in my women's Bible study. One woman, now in marriage counseling, said she regrets she didn't work on better communication. She now knows it hurt her husband that she didn't *greet* him when he got home. They both worked, but she got home a little earlier, and she'd just yell 'Hi, I'm in the other room' when he came in. He wanted her to come to the door...but there you go again with communication problems— he never told her.

"When Scott comes home I take his coat and hang it up, put his briefcase in the corner, give him a hot or cold drink depending on the weather. And he does the same for me. I love it when I'm at a night meeting at church, say, and I come home and the porch light is on and there are Scott and Meghan calling out, 'Hi, Mom!' I think you should welcome members of the family, even if they've just been to the store."

Part of the re-entry problem is what we might call the "Colliding Worlds" effect. All day, spouses have been in separate worlds, doing different things, sometimes many miles apart. Suddenly, boom! partners reunite and the worlds run into each other. Fran Meyers uses another metaphor: "I feel Scott comes home with this sort of film on him from his day. It's so hard to get through. You can tell the facts but not the feelings. But I don't want him to leave his feelings at work. I want to help so we can be a real couple, sharing in these struggles."

In his book *After the Wedding*, Philip Yancey shares the "reintroduction" concept practiced by one couple, the Gilbertsons. They made it a point early in their marriage to spend time talking about what they'd learned or how they'd changed that day. Even if Steve, who worked late as a social worker, came home at midnight, Jody would get up to review the day's events with him. Likewise, Steve would get up early to have breakfast with Jody before she went off to work. "We noticed that schedules could drive apart," Steve told Yancey. "You can always make up lost sleep; a slipping marriage is harder to recover."

Re-entry is hard for children as well, who need our time if they haven't seen us all day. I try to give my daughter a good dose of what we call "Mommy Time"—playing, reading, going for a walk. That usually satisfies her, and she goes off to play while I relax with my husband and start dinner. (Unless, of course, I relax and *he* starts dinner.)

## Do You, Nick, Take This Job...

Nick Vassilakis is very good at what he does. He is a rising star in the intensely competitive world of advertising. His specialty is creating upscale slice-of-life magazine ads; he works with passion and precision, and his work has won a number of industry awards.

He also works a lot, "seventy-five hours a week during the worst craziness." Most Saturday mornings are spent at the office. He feels pressured by the grind but, with Greek fatalism, shrugs it off. "What are you going to do? It's the nature of my work, carved-in-stone deadlines. I freelance, too, and you don't want to jeopardize your relationship with valued clients.''

Nick's wife, Tina, works part-time as a labor and delivery nurse. She puts in some evening and weekend hours; they juggle sitters and schedules—and they don't see much of each other. Things came to a head recently when Tina had to cope with a sick child, increased hours at the hospital, and a broken washing machine. She had had enough. She shouted at Nick, "You've *got* to stop leaving me with all this stuff!" Nick replied, "You think I *like* going into the office all the time?" Tina paused. "I think you do," she said.

After eleven years of marriage, Tina knows her husband pretty well. A relentless perfectionist, Nick thrives on work. Even when he's home, he's working. It's taken him six months to put a deck on the back of their house because he hasn't had the time to do it exactly right.

Nick wonders if he fits the classic "workaholic" profile; he also wonders if that's good or bad. Some workaholics, mostly men, do neglect their marriages, sometimes to the point of divorce. At the same time, says one fifty-year-old executive, "You can't put your family first and still be a success on the job. That happened to two guys I know—and they got fired." This executive adores his wife and children. But he also recognizes, with hard-eyed realism, that a man or woman who really wants to break into top management needs to be *at* the job long hours—and needs to be *thinking* about the job the rest of the time.

Both this executive and his wife, and Nick and Tina, have developed tacit agreements that, often, the job will come first. Tina knows what makes Nick happy—work. However, she will call him to account when necessary. Once, during a particularly hectic period at the office, Nick worked until two in the morning. When he came home, Tina sat him down and spelled it out: *no more*. "It's not the source of tension it used to be for us," Nick says. "We've learned to understand what makes the other person happy."

## Help Your Marriage—Go to Work!
There's a cliché in Christian circles that goes something like this: A celebrity—athlete, business-man, entertainer—says earnestly, "I've learned to keep my priorities straight. I put God first, my wife second, children third, job last." The irony is, he wouldn't have got where he is if he always put his job last.

And the question is, why would he want to? As Nick Vassilakis and my executive friend have discovered, work is fun. Sometimes—many times—it's more fun than vacations, or even home. Home is where you have to pick up after somebody. At work, if you're in a white-collar or professional position, someone is picking up after you—and answering your phone, paying you for your ideas and making you laugh.

And you don't have to be a CEO or advertising hotshot to enjoy your job. I once had a job stuffing envelopes. I didn't love the work, and the pay was negligible. But the other women and I talked and joked, and I looked forward to going to work every morning.

Certainly the work routine exacerbates the sense of the daily grind. But can work *benefit* a marriage? Evelyn Eaton Whitehead and James Whitehead, counselors at Notre Dame, think so: "Who works, at what kind of job, under what conditions, with what demands and what rewards—these issues help define the kind of marriage we have." By implication, then, work that is challenging and rewarding can help define a marriage positively. Work does not have to drain the lifeblood of a marriage. It can feed it. (When work is not going well, or there is no work, the marriage can suffer. Study after study has shown that unemployment, usually the husband's, can strain marriages literally to the breaking point.)

Work plays a large role in our self-esteem. As recently as twenty years ago social scientists and futurists were predicting a leisure boom, when work would occupy a minor part of Americans' days. It never happened, partly because we need to say: "I work at something. I *am* something."

Many couples talk about work, thereby merging their two worlds. Jim Donovan says, "Cathy has a good sense about people, so I've called her in the middle of the day to role-play with her a difficult phone call I had to make. She said I was doing it all wrong. I followed her advice and it went better than I expected."

Judy and Dale Hammond also discuss work at home. "I know the people Dale works with," Judy says. "I know their families, so it's not as if it's so foreign. He doesn't usually ask my advice," she says with a grin, "but I give it anyway!"

Worlds can be completely merged. Phyllis and Augie Morelli, who run a Chicago-area deli renowned for its titanic sandwiches, say flatly, "Our real success is our togetherness." The Morellis have been married thirty-three years. Augie told writer Gregg Lewis, "Every day someone asks us how we can work together day after day and still be married. I tell 'em it's the most wonderful thing in the world to be working with the best friend you'll ever have in your entire life."

It works for the Morellis. Other couples say working so closely together would drive them crazy. But, as Fran Meyers says, "The times Scott and I have been closest have been when we worked on shared projects."

### Disbanding the Corporation

We probably can't completely escape the jaws of the daily routine. There's just too much stuff to do—unless we want the Health Department to slap a "Condemned" sign on our front door, unless we want our kids to live in front of the TV, eating nothing but Goldfish crackers and drinking Kool-Aid, unless we want to be fired from our jobs. In a way, the daily grind is a reverse compliment: we're responsible enough, successful enough, involved enough to *have* a demanding routine.

Gee, aren't we lucky?

Consider the alternative, however. I've been there: no work, no marriage, no house, no kids, few friends; nothing to do but type up résumés and read a lot. Now, I cannot imagine having so much free time. I've smelled the flowers—now I'm busy planting them. As we all are, together with our life's partners.

---

## A Few Small Victories

Marriage, Inc., is a frustration and a reality. But is it unalterable? No. Here are a few suggestions that may help ease the pressure.

◆ Part of "to-do list stress" comes from the fact that nothing ever seems to get done. Don't let chores overwhelm you. Think of *one* job that is do-able—

29

then do it. It's important, though, that this be a task that will stay completed for a while—unlike, say, laundry or dishes. And it helps if it's something visible. For example, we painted our front door. We've been wanting to do it for months; now it's finished and looks nice and we don't feel like such terminal procrastinators.

◆ Make a weekly—not a daily—to-do list, suggests Mary Lee Harrell. That way you can be more realistic about what can be accomplished.

◆ Ask someone to help with a job for which you feel inadequate. Jack Donovan had a friend work with him to build a tool shed. Jack says it forced him to complete the task. In addition, they had a good time doing it, and he saved money.

◆ Whistle while you work. Several couples try to perform chores together, combining couple time with grind time. Turn up the music and dust along with Bach or Bruce Springsteen.

◆ Try to keep written lists rather than nag each other. (And don't nag each other to look at the list.) Cross items off as you do them.

◆ Consider what's really important. One woman we know believes that a clean house is a sin. You don't have to go that far, but it's easy, especially for working parents, to get so caught up in "accomplishing" things that we overlook our children.

◆ When possible, involve the kids in the chores. Although the supervisory role may make your life even more complicated, they'll feel good about pitching in. They may even get something done.

◆ Take Sunday seriously. It should *not* be just another

day of shopping, yard chores, office work. For Christians, Sunday is regarded as a day of rest. It's more than tradition. It's an acknowledgment that God made human beings, not machines, and we all need time to rest. At the same time, meeting with other people to worship God provides healing and refreshment.

◆ Allow yourselves small breathing moments. Anyone can take ten minutes to sip iced tea while watching birds in the back yard or go for a quick stroll around the neighborhood. (This is especially important in easing the work-to-home transition.) Some couples get up early for coffee, prayers and planning the day's schedule.

◆ Share your frustrations, but don't gripe incessantly.

◆ Know thyself. I have to clean every week; otherwise I feel as if I'm living in filth. My husband and I clean together. We have a small house, so it's done in half a day. It's a choice we've made.

◆ Realize that you aren't the only person whose house is sometimes (or often) a mess, whose bank account gets overdrawn, whose car looks like a dumpster with an engine. We tend to see other people, close friends included, at their best. Similarly, they see the best side of *us* and may even envy our efficiency and effortless achievement. The truth, of course, lies under the surface (or stuffed in a closet).

Chapter Three

# Will We Ever Have Enough Money?

Me:
*I have a question. How do people
make it these days?*

Financial-expert friend:
*There's a short answer to that: They
don't.*

Lynne and Paul Randle have three children ages five
and under. They live in a small house in a modest
neighborhood. Paul is a typographer; Lynne teaches
piano. This year they've been hit with major medical
expenses—for a new baby, surgery for Paul, dental
work for Lynne. They rent out their basement and
avoid credit cards. The children wear hand-me-
downs; the Randles recently bought a used car with
80,000 miles on it. "It's a V-8," Paul says. "It'll go
over 100,000."

Because of their frugal lifestyle they have been able
to make ends meet—barely, but they've met. Now,

however, they are seriously mulling a move back to Lynne's home state of Tennessee, where two-hundred-dollar monthly heating bills and two-thousand-dollar annual property taxes would seem like unimaginable nightmares. The Randles, like many middle-class couples, are teetering on the line between comfort and catastrophe.

You don't have to be poor to be budget conscious. Cameron Douglas, a financial counselor, now earns in the six figures. "When I earned only a quarter of what I now make, Nancy and I had to budget; we had no money. Now, when I'm making more, we still have to budget. I see it all the time with couples: the more you make, the more you spend."

The more people you talk to, the more you wonder: Does anyone in their thirties and early forties feel like they're making it financially? And is this unease just yuppie "poor talk," or are today's wage earners really less well off than the previous generation?

First, a look at some numbers:

◆ In the 1950s housing costs absorbed 18 per cent of a family's income. Today the figure is 43 per cent.
◆ The average income of a male wage earner has declined 21 per cent since 1972.
◆ The "median of the median"—the middle fifth of the middle class—now accounts for just 16.7 per cent of the gross national income, according to the Census Bureau. That's the lowest percentage on record.
◆ Household income showed a net real *decline* of $150 in 1988, due largely to rising taxes.
◆ The typical car on the road is now eight years old. A new car costs an average of $15,000.

These are worrisome figures, and they provide statistical warrant for gut feelings. In 1984 Ronald

Reagan asked America if it was "better off today" than in 1980. America answered with a resounding yes.

But while the economy has shown real strength in what experts call "the longest peacetime recovery" since World War II, the landscape is dotted with patches of unease, the sense that "morning in America" dazzles with artificial light. The federal budget deficit has reached gigantic proportions; America has the lowest personal savings rate and highest consumer debt in the world; a portion of the Reagan recovery was fueled by foreign investment. It has even been argued that the illegal drug trade drains off massive amounts of cash from the economy.

People are hurting. A decade ago $40,000 would have seemed a princely annual income; now it is not enough to qualify for most mortgages. It's beyond the scope of this book to establish conclusive connections between the federal deficit and the Randles' plight. But something is happening. "I don't know how anyone saves these days," is a lament I've heard more than once. Yet save we must.

Experts predict that the Baby Boom generation may not be able to count on the comfortable retirement many of our parents are now enjoying. No law requires private employers to provide pension benefits, and as the Baby Boomers move into retirement age the supply of pension dollars may not meet the demand. Social Security won't fill the void.

Those of us just entering middle age had better stay healthy on our way to our pinched sunset years. If we get sick, we can't count on our group insurance picking up the tab; only twenty-eight per cent of employers now provide full medical insurance, and this percentage is continually decreasing. The rest require their workers to contribute out of their own pockets.

## Ozzie Nelson Never Worked

Sylvia Nasar, writing in *Fortune* magazine several years ago, contended that there *is* a degree of "poor talk" in the complaints of today's younger couples. We suffer, she says, "from an acute variant on the timeless theme of high expectations. The reach that exceeds the grasp has always earmarked the middle class."

In America, at least, every generation reaches higher. The house I live in, for example, was built around 1920. It has tiny closets and not many of them. When we were looking at the house with our realtor, I asked him, "Where did people put their clothes?" "They didn't have many in those days," he said. "The man owned a workday suit and a Sunday suit. The woman had maybe three dresses. That was about it."

Such amenities as air conditioning, dishwashers and color TV are now viewed as basic needs. New houses always have more than one bathroom, and most cars have automatic transmission. Yesterday's luxury mutates into today's necessity. And it all costs money.

Another factor enters the feeling-poor equation, however. Most of us grew up in relatively comfortable circumstances in the 1950s, which begin to look like the halcyon decade of affluence. Families *could* make it on one income. We remember new cars every two years, summer vacations to the seashore or the national parks, few requests denied. My own childhood memories are burnished with a mellow glow of ease and comfort—ballroom dancing lessons with a dowager instructor, a twice-weekly cleaning woman, leg of lamb for dinner and the *Christmases!* "We got so much for Christmas it was almost embarrassing," recalls Tim, who grew up in a similarly privileged environment.

Tim, who often feels poor even though both he and his wife are well-educated professionals, continues: "I think one of the reasons we feel poor and want more is because our parents generated those expectations in us. They assumed we'd go to college, be achievers."

We also assume that someday we will be able to afford the same sort of five-bedroom home many of us spent our childhoods in. With maids and an occasional landscaping service. And still be able to give our kids the Lincoln Log sets, Madame Alexander dolls and real planetariums we remember spilling out from under the tree on Christmas morning. All this without working twelve-hour days—or working at all. Looking back, I remember a feeling of spacious and unhurried ease about those days. Mothers led Scout troops and went to Garden Club meetings and organized charity fundraisers. Fathers took the train to the office and were home promptly at six every night. (Television's Ozzie Nelson didn't even appear to have a job.) Couples even seemed to socialize more.

Somehow people seemed to have both money *and* time—a feat which in the nineties seems wondrous. Does anyone, anywhere, live like this anymore?

### How Do People Make It These Days?
No doubt some of our childhood memories have taken on the hue of myth—winters were always Currier-and-Ives snowy and summer went on and on. But, I think, life *was* good in those postwar years.

And the answer to the above question—Does anyone live like this any more?—is this: We try to.

The legacy of the easy fifties has left many of us indelibly printed with the idea that this is how life is supposed to be. We're supposed to live in suburban comfort, drive a nice car, work at white-collar jobs. Everyone is scared to death of looking poor. Because of this fear, many couples have stretched themselves to the breaking point.

I once asked Joyce Chambers, our daughter's baby sitter and a friend of ours, if I could pay her with a postdated check. "You know how it is," I said with a weak smile.

"Oh, I sure do," she said. "We feel like we're not making it. Lou's been talking about taking a second job—yet he comes home late every night as it is. I really don't want to go to work full-time because Emma's still just two. We've been looking at houses but can't find anything in our price range in this area. I don't know what we're going to do."

The Chamberses have four children, no dining room and an unreliable car they bought secondhand. Like an increasing number of families, they've never owned a new car. Joyce, a lovely redhead, wishes she could buy some new clothes. They feel trapped by their middle-income lifestyle in an increasingly expensive area. They, too, ask how others make it.

It is true that 90 per cent of the world would regard our standard of living with awe. But, rightly or wrongly, we don't compare ourselves to the teeming millions dying in the *favelas* outside São Paulo or the children of Manila forced into prostitution. We compare ourselves to the neighbor down the street, the friend in church, the colleague at work. In a perceptive election-year column in the *Chicago*

*Tribune* a few years ago, reporter Jon Margolis described American society as a collection of "tribes"—with their own rituals, dress, animosities. We judge ourselves against others in our tribe.

Writer Janis Long Harris tells the story of her friends Brent and Karen. Brent has experienced a series of career reversals which have set their family on the road of downward mobility. Karen has been forced to work full-time as a nurse. Both in their forties, Brent and Karen are not living the "lifestyle they expected to be living at this stage of their lives." Harris quotes Karen: "In my mind, I'm still a middle-class person. But when my surroundings and material possessions descend further and further to the lower-class end of things, I have to decide, Who am I, really?"

Most of their friends are upscale professionals. Among them, Karen says, "We always...feel odd man out."

Even among churchgoing couples, the pressures of the tribe can take their toll. John and Barb Gates, for example, are active in a church in one of Detroit's wealthiest suburbs. John feels a degree of discomfort with the church because, he says, most of the parishioners are well-to-do and the Gateses are not. Even the gatherings of the young couples' group tend to be expensive affairs.

### Does It Matter?

Is it right for a church-group outing to cost fifty dollars? Should the religious community practice its preachments? Or are warnings such as "The love of money is the root of all evil" hopelessly out of touch?

It would seem out of touch, looking back at the eighties. In a provocative book, *Circus of Ambition*, author John Taylor asserts that the decade saw a fundamental reshaping of American attitudes toward money: " notion that money is good as a central tenet of the culture... At its center was the belief that the accumulation of wealth is morally and even spiritually virtuous... Money was good."

Yet I would argue that there's a deep strain of ambivalence toward money in the American psyche. We may admire and even envy the lifestyle of a wealthy junk-bond king like Michael Milken, but we're happy when he's indicted and believe no one should make half a billion dollars a year. We cheer on our favorite baseball and football players, but we wonder why they earn in the six figures while we struggle to make ends meet.

And so, as we compare our station in life with others', many of us also ponder just how healthy it is to be worrying about these things at all. We wonder if the lifestyle we've chosen hasn't gotten impossibly cumbered and complicated.

Have we become hopelessly materialistic? Do we need to develop a broader, more spiritual perspective on life? I put the question to Dr. Louis McBurney, a Colorado psychiatrist who with his wife, Melissa, runs a counseling and retreat center for clergy and their spouses. "Is it wrong, from a Christian perspective, to want to live in a decent neighborhood and send your children to good schools?" I asked.

"No," said Dr. McBurney, "but it has to be balanced with other concerns. It can't be your *only* concern. We're too isolated from the world's needs. Doing something for the poor is very healthy for a marriage. And it creates a way for us not to feel so bad about what we have."

### Enough Is Enough

Some couples, of course, feel as if they have very

little—which, as we have seen, can be a subjective judgment indeed. When is enough enough? How can we achieve the feeling that we're where we want to be–we have enough? Dr. McBurney says, "I think it's a matter of being conscious and acting intentionally. A couple has to stop occasionally and ask themselves, 'What do we *really* want and need?'"

And that is where the issues blur. Strictly speaking, no one literally *needs* anything save food, shelter, clothing and medical care. But, as psychologist Abraham Maslow has pointed out with his famous "hierarchy of needs" theory, as a society becomes more affluent, needs evolve. When people no longer worry about basic sustenance, they move on to needs for fulfillment, life opportunities and so on.

I could live without a microwave oven. But now that I have one, I find that the time it occasionally saves in cooking is a gift—it frees me to spend more time with my daughter. On the other hand, my Cuisinart gathers dust in an upper cupboard because it's too complicated and time-consuming to figure out. I thought I needed a food processor. I found out differently.

The point, as McBurney said, is to pause and reflect as a couple: Are we where we want to be? If not, what will it take to get there? Know yourselves. Not everyone is willing to drive a fifteen-year-old beater for the sake of living more simply. There's nothing inherently virtuous in poverty. But a couple should ask themselves: Do we "need" a brand-new car or would a late-model used car do as well?

Money—and not having it—can gnaw at a marriage. Financial worry is an insidious kind of beast. But it is true that money isn't everything. Keeping up appearances isn't worth it. Relentless striving isn't even healthy. But your relationship with your mate *is* vitally important. Whatever the decisions you make about money, however you choose to set your priorities—keep in mind what, and who, comes first.

The problem with constant striving is just that: it never ends. I recently read about a young mother who felt she "had to" work full-time to support their family's lifestyle—even though her husband earned close to six figures! When is enough enough?

We hear it a lot, but at some point we do have to look at money with an eternal perspective. Things break and wear out. Vacations are pleasant, but all too fleeting. Providing a comfortable home for our family is important—but we can become enslaved by the continual maintenance and seemingly never-ending mortgage payments. I like the response of the old Catholic priest to a parishioner who was complaining because his new car had got a flat tire: "Never love anything that doesn't love you back."

I admit: I like my things—a radically pared-down, "simple lifestyle" doesn't appeal. However, things don't love you back; besides, they need dusting and clipping and sorting, and too many things add to the solid-waste problem. Who needs it?

Beyond that, there's the deeper question of what really matters in the scheme of things. The Bible is clear about the place money and material possessions are to have in our lives. God does not demand we take a vow of poverty (although some Christian thinkers would say yes, he does). But...we can't serve him *and* our material strivings both. Abundance is to be shared, not hoarded. We who have been blessed with relative good fortune are to attend to the cries of the needy. And at some point, we have to call a halt to our yen for more.

We hear this so often that the various statements Scripture makes concerning money tend to go in one ear and out the other. But we'd better listen. In our restless age, contentment is an enviable, precious thing. I've known a few—a very few—truly contented people in my life. I've wanted to be like that; as I get older I'm trying to find out how to be like that. And what I have found is that the universal human yearning that there must be more to life than what we see around us is not satisfied by still more consumer durables, but in acknowledging the God who made us. The inner peace that comes from setting life on this foundation makes it possible for me to say that I do have all I need. And then I feel truly rich.

**Money, Emotions and What One Couple Did**
True, the bills still keep coming in. And there are specific things couples can do about money—and not having it. Part of many people's frustration about money arises from the feeling of darkness at the end of the tunnel—no way out, short of drastic solutions such as changing jobs or moving or even declaring bankruptcy. Most money books are geared to people who already *have* money, so they tend to be unhelpful. Money *is* important, and there's nothing wrong with legitimate concern about it—to a point.

The concern, however, should translate into action. Continual agonizing is unproductive. And too many couples agonize in isolation, keeping up the exhausting task of maintaining a facade. People tend not to share their financial woes. But, says Hope Morrison, a forty-two-year-old who finally broke the silence, "Eventually you have to talk to someone. My husband did, and it made all the difference." The Morrisons, like many families, were uneasy about their credit-card and miscellaneous debt, which totaled about ten thousand dollars. "Not awful, when you read about some people's indebtedness," says Hope. "But we weren't comfortable; we were sick of seeing our money go to making those interest payments. It never seemed to end."

The Morrisons, after several years of pretending to be affluent, decided enough was enough. "We started getting all these overdraft notices from the bank," says Hope. "Third notices on bills. Even the mortgage check bounced. And Christmas was coming, and we didn't know how we were going to afford presents for anyone. I said to my husband, 'This is horrible. Something has to give.' I felt we were sliding toward financial ruin. Not only that, but we were both tired of having the same old money arguments over and over. I would nag; Lee would get defensive about not making enough money. The dynamics were really unhealthy. Yet here we were making about thirty-six thousand between us, and we don't care about a lavish lifestyle. We kept saying to each other, 'We should be making it.'"

Lee Morrison immediately agreed with his wife that they needed help. He secured loans from both family and close friends—"we had talked about getting one of those consolidation loans," he says, "but that seemed like trading one kind of slavery for another. But we knew we needed to get our creditors off our backs."

It wasn't easy for the Morrisons to open up about their financial plight, says Hope. "But once we did, we felt this huge relief. We were very selective about whom we went to, of course." They also shared their worries with a friend who runs his own business, a man they felt to be financially astute. He helped them set up a workable budget that enabled the Morrisons to set aside money for both savings and church and charitable contributions.

"We never tithed before," says Hope. "We tried to give what we could, of course; we believe it's important to give back to God. But we didn't think we could afford a tenth of our income. Now that we see where the money's going and have categories allocated, we can tithe. I wish we could do even more. Maybe someday."

Hope and Lee still wish they had more money. But they no longer think they hear the wolf stealthily approaching the door. "For the first time, we feel in control of our situation," Hope sums up. "But we couldn't have done it ourselves. And most important, we're not fighting about money anymore. Well, not much!"

---

## How to Deal with Feeling Poor

◆ Decide what your real priorities are. Is "owning more" really the best goal you could have? What about God, friends, family?

◆ Acknowledge how affluent you really are. We really do live in a wealthy nation, and even those of us who feel we are a disgrace to the neighborhood enjoy many good things over and above mere necessities.

◆ Don't let other people—or the media—determine your lifestyle. If you're truly content with less, pay no attention to the blandishments of glossy magazine ads or the decor of the Huxtable home. By the same token, if you enjoy the choices money offers, don't apologize—but do know when *you* have enough and your good fortune could benefit others. The point is to act intentionally.

◆ Stay out of stores as much as possible. Resisting the consumer society is not un-American. We don't need most of the stuff being hawked; it just has to be dusted. On the other hand, know when to give yourselves a modest splurge. Everyone should feel rich once in a while, if only by buying Haagen-Dazs instead of generic ice cream.

◆ Stop the hand-wringing. Feeling poor is like dieting. Dieting makes you overly preoccupied with food; poor talk makes you overly preoccupied with money. Agree with your spouse to stop the endless discussions.

◆ Know that you have choices. Money, ultimately, is neither an evil nor a god. It's a thing, a tool at *your* disposal. Choices do have consequences; for example, a larger house means a bigger monthly payment and less money left over for something else.

◆ Laugh with your spouse and other friends. I know a man who is always joking about feeling poor (and I think of him as quite successful). If the only people you talk to are tiresome paragons of monetary prudence, you will be miserable. Believe me: you are not alone.

◆ Pray about your situation. A spiritual perspective on money and your money concerns provides a needed balance to what can become an unhealthy overemphasis on the material. And God answers prayer—not necessarily with a "miracle" check but by helping you to adjust your lifestyle and find riches and fulfillment in relationship with him and with other people.

Chapter Four

# Can Marriage Survive Children?

*There sat Saul and Marshall, playing
chess on the coffee table. In the dining
room Rebecca was laying out the
silver. Naomi was cutting paper-doll
dresses. Ruth was painting
watercolors. Joseph was running his
electric train.... Every hand, every
head, every mouth made a big or little
motion.... Everything was there and
everything was working.*

Ray Bradbury


*There are two ways to travel: first
class and with children.*

Robert Benchley


Which is the reality—Bradbury's cozy, pre-
television portrait or Benchley's acerbic travel
wisdom? Regardless, most of us choose to have

children. If we cannot, we seek to adopt or we find other people's children to fold into our lives.

In some critical ways, you cannot separate a marriage from the resulting children. Traditionally, producing descendants was the reason for getting and staying married. It's less true now, but most people still feel that the fusing of their love and genes into a new creation completes the circle.

Having kids is hard. Having kids is easy. One or two is all you can realistically handle. Have a quiverful. Today there are almost as many opinions about children, and their effect on a marriage, as there are Barbie doll clothes. And in this area, more than almost any other, there are few right and wrong answers—only searching questions, leaps of faith and big chunks of love.

## Skin to Skin

I know one couple who, when they decided to start a family and abandon male contraceptives, called their lovemaking "skin to skin." After several years of marriage, they were ready to complete the circle. After a few months of skin-to-skin closeness, they did conceive and went on to produce a healthy, much-wanted baby girl.

It's not that tidy for all husbands and wives. Deborah and Marc Fox waited fourteen years to have a child—and it was not because they had trouble conceiving. I have a memory of the Foxes at a church picnic, standing hand in hand watching boys play baseball at a nearby diamond. "Deb and Marc can't have kids. How sad," I thought at the time. Months later Deborah announced her pregnancy. "She finally got pregnant after trying so many years!" I thought happily.

Wrong. They didn't think they wanted to have

children. "Marc wasn't really interested," Deb said recently, keeping one eye on her toddler daughter as we talked in the children's room of the library. "Having children was a threat to him. He thought, 'We've got our lives all set—why do this?'

"And I was unwilling to have children for a long time because I had grown up with some unhealthy family models. Marc and I really needed to work on some issues in our marriage first, like trust and vulnerability. Then I started wanting children, and Marc didn't. But he finally decided that God wanted him to be a loving husband...and Deborah wants children...so that's part of loving."

Today Marc is not only a loving husband, he's an exemplary father who involves himself as much as he can in the care of his daughter, Rachel.

In the Foxes' case, the long, tortuous road to a planned pregnancy came out at a sunny clearing. But what of unplanned pregnancies? Are there any long-term effects on a marriage when the kids come too soon? Or too frequently?

Mary and Peter MacIntosh married young—and poor. Two years later their first child came along. "Jenni wasn't planned," Mary said. "I honestly think that's one reason money has always been our biggest problem—we've now been married fourteen years and things are still really tight. We had only one year when both of us were working full-time. So we didn't start off with anything set aside, unlike young couples today who earn $70,000 between them and have no kids and rent an apartment to save money for a house."

At the same time, she acknowledges, "Jenni made us a family"— indeed, Jenni helped their young marriage grow up.

The MacIntoshes have almost no time to

themselves, not with three children at stages ranging from just-out-of-diapers to just-into-boys. They badly need a new car, but with a family of five, they're looking for a minivan—not cheap. Their house is too small. Mary will be past fifty by the time the nest empties. But she has an air of serenity; she is at peace with their choices. Both Mary and Peter wanted three children. They continue to cherish those children, even if they began arriving a little earlier than expected.

Whether children come too early or too late, there's a scent of dropping-out-of-heaven about them, a sense that something in one's personal cosmos has been forever jolted.

### So That's What You Look Like!

Like most mothers fortunate enough to be reasonably alert for their children's births, I can still recall, in bright detail, nearly every minute. The strange, strange feeling of water suddenly soaking the mattress in the middle of the night. Grabbing a banana before leaving for the hospital. (Even though I knew I wasn't supposed to eat, I was starving.) My husband's Thermos of coffee breaking in the parking lot. The nurse taking my thumbprint. Searing back pain. The feeling of stepping outside and watching myself have a baby, as if I were simultaneously posing and running a camera.

More than anything, though, I remember this: When the doctor eased my baby out and showed her to me, perfectly formed, eyes wide, not crying, my instant reaction was, So *that's* what you look like! I'd been getting to know this child for nine months, unseen but still familiar. I felt as if I was hugging a pen pal I'd been writing to for years.

She looked like her parents. But she also looked, remarkably, like herself. "What are you going to name her?" the nurse asked. I looked at my daughter. "That's Amanda," I said. Not "We'll name her Amanda," but "*That's* Amanda." As if that had been her name since the moment of quickening. Of course. How could she be anything else?

Our further acquaintance with her only strengthened our initial sense of a person both fresh and finished. And that, more than anything, is the awe babies bring to a marriage. I know all about the broken sleep; my daughter nursed forever and often. I know about the endless Lean Cuisine dinners because neither parent wants to cook. I know how husband and wife turn into sexless buddies like Garrison Keillor's Minnesotans: "When they go to bed, they sleep."

But I also recall an ineffable sense of wonder and delight as I would sit on the couch holding our baby, while my husband sat with his arm around us both. We'd look at her. Then we'd look at each other. And one of us would say, "We did that. I can't believe it."

Having a baby may be the closest human beings ever come to knowing how it feels to be God, who sees that it is good. It is a remarkable act of shared creation, and it is one of the most powerful forces for bonding that a couple can know. Studies have shown that the divorce rate drops precipitously when there are infants in the home. Not surprising: how can you abandon a beloved creation? Or abandon the co-creator?

## Louisa May Alcott Was Right

Yet studies also show, consistently, that marital satisfaction declines after the children come. Louisa

May Alcott never married, but she knew about family dynamics. In *Little Women*, after Meg gives birth to twins, she and her husband, John, drift apart. John rarely talks to her in the evening and spends more time than she'd like at the home of a young, childless couple. She feels matronly, frumpy, neglected. When she complains to her mother, wise Marmee gently reminds her that John needs her too, that she is to be a wife as well as a mother.

When I first read this as a girl of eight or nine, I thought, "Shouldn't they just be glad to have babies? Wouldn't it make them even happier?" But Louisa Alcott knew what she was talking about. Children can compromise marital happiness—or at least dull its edge.

The instinct to turn our attention to our children is powerful, even primal; every species puts its young first. Yet putting the children first generally means putting the marriage last. The marriage is expected to fend for itself, whereas children need concentrated attention.

Kids mean less money, less time, more noise, more mess and more confusion. They consume enormous amounts of physical and emotional energy—energy, then, that is not available to one's spouse.

Is there any solution to all this? Most of the couples I talked to say they endure the tensions as a tradeoff for the joys of having children. One father of four summed it up: "I don't think we do handle it." This couple almost never go out together. Children, including a new baby, are constantly underfoot. There's a sense of resignation—waiting it out.

In twelve years of raising children, the Mac-Intoshes have been away overnight only twice. "We'd kill for some time alone," Mary says wistfully. "Unfortunately, Peter's parents, who live nearby, won't baby-sit. So we go out to dinner every four months or so. We try to find time to talk after the children are in bed." Now, though, with the children getting older, that hour becomes later and later. "How do I deal with it? By realizing that everything passes, I guess. But my father once said to me, 'You only have your children for a short time—then they're gone. And then it's the two of you again.' "

## We, the Couple

The tricky, probably unanswerable question is this: Where does *we the couple* leave off and *we the family* begin? The distinction is a fine one. As parents it gives us great satisfaction to see our children content. On the other hand, it's important for children to know that their parents have a happy, productive marriage.

"The most important thing we can do for our children is build a good marriage relationship," the experts say. But what does that really mean? Love your kids by leaving them often to go out partying? By locking the master-bedroom door after nine? ("We're helping you by working on our marriage, dear.")

Like so much else, it's a question of proportion. The fact is that, often, children do have more immediate needs than spouses. A hungry baby can't wait; neither can a child with a skinned knee. Children need, and deserve, respect and careful attention—a sense that their world is important.

My husband knows that if I listen to Amanda first, while she tells a story about "Paul who bleeded his head on the playground," she will be satisfied and run off to play. And the older she gets, the less she'll need my total attention. However, Fritz sometimes needs my total attention. So once my daughter is off to her pursuits, I can turn to him for *our* pre-dinner debriefing time, knowing that we won't be interrupted.

## What's Your Chaos Threshold?

Bob is a free-lance writer with an undependable income. He and his wife, who doesn't work outside the home, have six children, teenage to preschool. They recently bought a century-old farmhouse in desperate need of repair; they have undertaken much of the work themselves and the house is in a seemingly permanent state of rehabbing disorder. Occasionally Bob, like many free-lance professionals, goes through lean times when the jobs don't come in. Then the renovation gets put on hold, and the disorder worsens.

Bob and his wife have a high tolerance for chaos. I could not live like that.

Jeanine, on the other hand, has one five-year-old and wonders about having another child. Highly committed to her career, Jeanine works part-time as a community-college instructor. She and her husband, who owns his own business, have weekly cleaning help. She is organized and efficient; she does not thrive on chaos.

Sandy calls herself a "cruiser." Because she is home-schooling her four children, the kids are always around (while her husband works long hours at the office). Sandy is unflappable. I have watched her hang wallpaper with kids literally crawling underfoot, and not once did she snap at them. Her most characteristic gesture is a shrug; she never seems hurried or harassed. She agrees she has a high chaos tolerance. Yet at the same time—and possibly *because* of this tolerance—she, too, is efficient and capable.

Three parents; three choices; three different ways of coping. How well couples deal with the early childhood years seems to be directly related to their chaos threshold—and *how much they know* about that threshold. Jeanine realizes that she needs a relatively well-ordered life and has chosen commensurately. Sandy knows she has the temperament required to handle a complicated and noisy existence. Bob, who has been married for about twenty years, knows his tolerance levels too.

I could not live like Bob. I would like to be a bit more like Sandy. I'm closest to Jeanine. No one way is "better." The challenge for couples is to be aware of their chaos thresholds and order their lives accordingly. The number of children we have, the kind of house we buy, the distance we live from our job, the kind of work we do—these things all bear on the chaos we live with. And, for the most part, these are also things we have choices about.

## Running Away from Home

Bev and Jake Schoonover struggle both with the chaos factor and with the deeper questions of identity as individuals, as a couple and as a family. Married fifteen years, they have two children, eleven and ten. Jake, who with his brothers owns a chain of drugstores in Wisconsin, loves being the good-guy dad and conscientious local businessman—most days. But he has been doing this as long as he and Bev, a travel agent, have been married. At times he wonders what other opportunities beckon, away from Milwaukee and cases of nasal spray and junk-jewelry earrings.

Jake loves to travel, sing, act, eat in new restaurants. Having children, he says, has limited his options: "I feel like I owe it to my kids to live a middle-class life. If we didn't have children, we'd go back to Greenwich Village, where we met, or I'd chuck it all and go to the Caribbean and open a restaurant. But with kids you plug away. Sometimes, though, I do feel very bored—and boring."

This "who am I, really?" issue is peculiar to our generation. Even as we move into our forties we sometimes feel like impostor grown-ups, like one of those carnival attractions that have paintings of old-fashioned people with holes cut out to stick your head through. While we are anxious to be competent and loving parents, we also don't want to be Ward Cleaver, who was born in a suit and tie.

Some, like the Schoonovers, feel the tension more keenly than others. Bev is an intense, creative person, almost wired with physical energy. She says they walk the nonconformist/solid citizen tightrope uneasily: "At the risk of embarrassing the children, we try to be ourselves within the context of a middle-class existence. We're considered avant-garde and artsy by the standards of this community, which is mostly German and Dutch and very conservative." The Schoonovers live in a contemporary house, have a hot tub, wear bright clothes, enjoy Thai cuisine. They love going to plays and films, and they have many friends in Milwaukee's artistic community. Bev's job enables them to take frequent trips.

At the same time, Bev sings in the church choir. Jake is a respected businessman. Their two sons are in gifted-level classes at school. They keep up with extended family and manage their household with the Dutch zeal for organization. And they are fine, instinctive parents.

But they try to remember that they are more than that—and even more than just "the Schoonovers," a two-headed entity. As a result, because they have not disappeared into marriage, they have one of the strongest, most resilient marriages I know.

### "I Feel Like We Have a Freak Family"

So far we've looked at couples with healthy, bright kids. What happens, though, when a child is seriously flawed—physically handicapped, learning-disabled, incurably hostile? What happens when much of your time is spent in the school counselor's office hearing things like "I'm sorry. Your son is hyperactive"? When night after night you're bone-exhausted from lifting your child from bed to bath to wheelchair to car and back again? When you face the future of a child who will live with you forever because she will never really grow up?

For parents of children who need them so desperately, there is no room to worry about "finding oneself," tripping over Lego on the floor, carving out quality couple time. Such things seem frivolous indeed.

Emily Mathias was an infant when she contracted meningitis. Night after night her mother, Betty, prayed over her hospital bed. Emily did recover—sort of. She is now a tall, striking thirteen-year-old. But there is something wrong with Emily's brain. The right front area does not function very well. She comes across, Betty says, as "borderline retarded." Emily laughs inappropriately, flares in anger, struggles with normal conversational interactions. "Her judgment is really bad," says Betty. "It's scary, because she's a pretty girl. I wonder what could happen."

Emily attends a private school where she receives specialized instruction. Her schooling costs the Mathiases thousands of dollars a year. While Ed

56

Mathias makes a good salary in a civil-service job, Emily's education and assorted medical needs drain off any excess.

Emily's handicap is particularly hard on Betty, who recently earned a doctorate in economics and was Phi Beta Kappa at an Ivy League school. Betty, no-nonsense and razor-quick, did not fail very much as a youngster. And, she admits, she has always valued intelligence. To compound Emily's difficulties, the Mathiases have two younger children who are bright, cooperative, appealing. Emily is the sore thumb, and everyone hurts because of it. The Mathiases' youngest daughter, nine-year-old Casey, once wept to her mother, "I feel like we're a freak family!" because someone had made fun of her awkward sister.

Emily is demanding, exhausting, at times unpleasant. "Neither one of us could singly handle it," Betty says of herself and Ed. "We cry together. We build each other up. One of us will have had all we can take, and the other will step in.

"However, I also see her as my salvation from 'smartness.' Without her I would have been this jerk of an arrogant person. The fact is, we're *all* in tremendous need. Emily helps us see the world the way I think God sees it.

"Sure, there's a lot of anger sometimes. Special arrangements have to be made. I can't leave the kids alone as much as I'd like. I can't ask Jane, my twelve-year-old, to deal with Emily. We have to set aside $7,500 each year to meet Emily's needs, so we've never been to Disney World, even though it's not that far from here. I once read something by the mother of a handicapped child where she compared having a disabled kid to planning a trip to Italy—and then you wind up in Holland. In other words, it's not better or worse; just different. Well, that's bull. It's not just different. It's *extremely* difficult."

Still, Emily is sensitive to another's pain. She can be remarkably loving and tender; I still remember a trip to visit the Mathiases, years ago. We pulled into the driveway. Emily, then about five, came running out and joyfully hurled herself into my arms. She had seen me only once before. I was deeply moved by the fierce affection of this strange, hurt child.

What hurts the most, says Betty, is the attitude of others. "Before we moved to Virginia, she was always in public schools. I think she was emotionally abused there. But the first day I picked her up at this new school, she got into the car and said, 'Mom, they *like* me here!'"

So the Mathiases weep together, learn compassion together, spell each other. They, like everyone else, search in vain for some time together. They're tired, generous people who don't know what the future holds for their daughter. But they have been careful not to let the sadness drive them apart. And they both have learned much about the world in the process.

### Law, Mercy and Teenagers
My daughter is only in kindergarten, but occasionally a flash of sauciness or rebelliousness ("When do *I* get to be the boss?" she'll demand after I've made a particularly onerous request) will make me wonder: Is this what it will be like for us in ten years?

One husband, the father of three teenagers, went through a particularly hard time with his oldest daughter, now in college. He and his wife could not agree on discipline, and they felt divided—and therefore conquered—by the girl. "It's like having a third adult in the house," he said. "A clever, manipulative adult coming into your marriage."

Finally his daughter emerged from her rough waters and is now contemplating marriage. The solution, for this couple, was simply to wait it out. Now, though, they have two teenage boys to worry about—the older of whom just announced he wants to join the Marines.

What is it about teenagers that strikes terror into parents' hearts and fosters all kinds of lame jokes about putting your children in cold storage until they're eighteen? Do teens have to trash a marriage?

I don't yet know what it's like to have adolescent children, but I was one once. I wonder how my parents felt when I would shut myself in my room for hours at a time, not doing homework, listening to Beatle records, and generally feeling moony and at odds with the world. Did they argue about me? Did they worry? Did they expect I would eventually grow out of it? I would not have wanted to parent me back then.

As Jim and Sally Conway, counselors and authorities on mid-life issues, point out, parents are often struggling with their own pressures at the same time their children are shedding childhood. Career tensions, the specter of aging, skyrocketing family expenses—the litany is a familiar one. Throw in an infirm grandparent or two, and the pressures can be well nigh intolerable. I know one fortyish woman who is simultaneously facing her daughter's wedding, her own parents' illnesses and a major job change. And she is paying for two children at expensive private colleges. This is not a sandwich—this is a vise.

Author Walter Wangerin, Jr., and his wife, Thanne, have four teenagers. Thanne dismisses the doomsayers. "I much prefer having teenagers to the preschool years. I *enjoy* my children now; they're good companions. I get tired of people saying, 'Wait until they're teenagers!' That's not fair.

"However, there are ways in which having teens is like having preschoolers all over again. Both ages take a lot of attention—and time away from your marriage."

Walter Wangerin observes that parents should periodically swap the mantles of "law" and "mercy"—strict legalist and good-guy bleeding heart. Both are needed for balance, but one parent should not be cast in the role of permanent heavy, while the other plays pushover-for-life. Thanne elaborates: "We decided which of us would be the sole disciplinarian of that child at that time. Matthew, for instance, went through a period recently of saying, 'I don't see why I have to be home for supper; it's so boring.' It was driving me up the wall; I had just had it. So I in effect backed off from being his mother, and Walt took over. We did the opposite with our daughter Talitha.

"What that does is relieve friction between the two of us. It has been a tremendous relief."

Despite the ravages rearing adolescents may bring, parents do need to remember that their teenagers, deep down, care about what they think; that they don't hate them—and that they are watching them. It is critical, therefore, that husbands and wives take care to model healthy examples for their children. "Every marriage is a marriage observed," writes reporter Miller Clarke, who surveyed a number of teens on what they had learned, for good or for ill, from their parents' marriages.

One young woman he interviewed said, "My parents went through several tough years in their marriage. There were times during my teens when I wondered if they wouldn't both be better off getting a divorce. But they didn't. They eventually worked through their problems to achieve a stronger marriage, and I'm extremely grateful that they've stuck it out. Their example convinced me that if two people are truly committed to each other, it's possible to survive almost anything. And that commitment is worth it."

When our daughter reaches her teenage years, I pray that my husband and I can show her that, even though many of her peers may come from broken homes—or homes where the walls ring with hostility or are silent with indifference—marriage *is* worth it. I hope that we will show her that loving, vital, laughing, courageous marriages are not the sole province of a screenwriter's fantasy. And I hope that she, too, will desire this for herself—because of what her mother and father showed her.

I think we can. I know many men and women who are doing just that with their teenagers. And their teenagers are paying attention.


## First Class, with Children

Science-fiction author Ray Bradbury tells the story of a man who labors for weeks to build a Happiness Machine. He finally puts a Rube Goldberg-like contraption together, only to have the thing fizzle out. In the end he watches his six children through the window of their house. Caught in the glow of the evening lamplight, they play and work and remind him: *This* is the real Happiness Machine.

Well, usually. Children, too, can break your heart, or just be there, bugging you again. But it is less what children do than that they *are*. There is the mystical connection of blood and DNA and generational bequest, those startling times when you look at a photograph of your great-grandfather and see your brother or your infant son.

But beyond blood, there is another kind of gift. I know a couple who struggled for seven years to have a child. Finally they abandoned the thousand-dollar-a-month fertility treatments and sought to adopt. Shortly thereafter, a baby boy was theirs.

I saw the mother this morning. Her dark eyes were radiant as she held her son, a dimpled creation with huge blue eyes and wide, gummed smile—one of those babies about whom you can say, "How adorable!" and actually mean it. There was something in this son's smile, something awesomely pure. It made me wonder if this is what the world was originally meant to look like.

A gift.

We create our children—but we are also given them. Through these amazing creatures we receive lessons in selflessness, vast amusement, occasionally unpleasant reminders of the worst in ourselves (because we see these blotches on our children). We project ourselves into the future, building a sort of invisible span into the unknown. Certainly, we learn marvelous new things about our spouse. We become both stronger and weaker, smarter and dumber. Our capacities are stretched; our emotions intensified. We sometimes stumble around half-crazy with exhaustion brought on by continual sacrifice for another. We learn new and humbling lessons in compromise and pragmatism ("Okay, you can have a third cookie").

Through it all, we are becoming far richer, far deeper men and women. Maybe even grown-ups after all—not sham parents. Real adults. And *that* helps our marriages. Another gift.

## Keeping Your Kids *and* Your Marriage Happy

There *is* life after birth—and it can be a much more rewarding, surprising and interesting life than couples imagine. Here are a few suggestions that may make being "married, with children" a little easier.

◆ Think positively. Don't focus on what you can't do, where you can't go, time and money you don't have. Be realistic about the pressures children bring, but avoid the current emphasis on children as interferences, burdens, time-stealers; it's unhealthy and counterproductive.

◆ Enjoy the world of children. Recently my daughter and I went to see the Disney animated film *The Little Mermaid*. I found the movie imaginative, funny, touching, engrossing—and enjoyed it more than any movie I'd seen in years. I love children's books. I love dropping by my daughter's school. We need kids in our lives, especially if we work all day with adults.

◆ If you and your spouse have differing tolerances, you may need to create separate spaces within your house—one for peace and one for disorder.

◆ Maintain an adults-only area. When toy clutter overflows a house, it suggests that children completely dominate the home and marriage, that adults' needs don't count. While I don't advocate segregating kids in their rooms to play (especially when quite young), I do recommend keeping one room, or part of one large room, clear of children's things. Kids will understand this and actually appreciate the idea of having their special corner.

◆ Reflect on and voice your appreciation for your spouse as a parent—his or her gifts, struggles, needs. Doing these things will increase your sense of being "in this together"—not just as two parents, but as a husband and wife who are also a father and mother.

◆ Enjoy your time together. One husband might talk to his wife while she changes clothes after coming home from work. Another couple might cook dinner together. If you have *no* time during the day, talk at night after you're in bed. When you have a Saturday afternoon free, resist the temptation to clean or run errands. Have fun.

◆ Pay attention to each other—and don't forget touching. Children are so demanding that it's easy to physically turn our backs on our spouses while we fuss over the kids. Greet each other after work; send each other off in the morning with love. *Remember* each other.

## Chapter Five

# Whatever Happened to Sex?

*It's like a steady diet of peanut butter
and jelly sandwiches.*

A wife of four years

Twenty years ago, sex was thick in the air. Clothes enticed. Music throbbed. Hormones danced. The world was for the young, and the feast included sex. Even if one did not partake—as many of us did not— the aura of youth and fun and possibility was enough.

Then the climate chilled. If the metaphor for the late sixties was a sunny Saturday afternoon in the park, with barefoot boys and girls playing Frisbee, watching free rock concerts and snuggling under trees, the metaphor for the early nineties is a raw Wednesday morning with raincoated men and women hurrying to catch the commuter train.

In the popular film *When Harry Met Sally*, Sally says that there is a dark little secret married people keep: There is *no* sex in marriage. True?

Not entirely. Yet the brightly colored, barefoot boys and girls of easy summer have turned into the safely beige, mostly married women and men of purposeful autumn. Arcing hormones have experienced a brownout. We're all too tired; and somehow it doesn't seem that much fun anymore.

## Is Married Sex a Contradiction in Terms?

If there's a middle-aged married couple out there who every night enjoy a rousing, laughing tumble, I didn't find them. Oh, people are having sex. But not as frequently, and possibly not with the same urgency and raw need that drove them in the honeymoon phase. Most people would identify with Carolyn, the wife of eighteen years who told me, "It's real hard to see my spouse as my lover. Brad and I have been successful at being good friends, but kids take away your privacy. He's exhausted; I'm exhausted. We haven't figured out a solution.

"I have a hard time thinking of myself as a sexual being. Recently I was sitting in the car waiting for one of the kids to get out of choir practice when suddenly the word *sex* came into my mind. And I thought, 'I remember that!' Sure, we can always do 'quickies'—but I need romance as well. Brad feels it too."

## Always on Call

This sense of being neutered pals, or partners in parenting and chores and not much else, begins when the first baby comes home from the hospital. It may ease up once the children are in school—*if* the children go to bed at a reasonable hour and if both of you are not wiped out from the day's demands. But as one mother of four teenagers said, once the children hit adolescence, your nights are more likely spent waiting up for them than waiting open-armed for your spouse.

"It's like you're always on call as a parent," said one father of two. "Even in sex, my wife is listening for the kids."

And sometimes you hear things. A friend tells this story: "One night my husband and I were enjoying some much-needed closeness, thinking our daughter was safely tucked in. It felt so good to be together.

"Then we heard her yell out, 'Mom-mee!' She sounded half asleep, so I suggested waiting. We did, and heard nothing more. But the damage was done. I had switched on my Vigilant Mother identity and shut off my Romantic Partner self. And Mom, as we all know, is sexless. My husband, too, lost interest."

In the morning of our union, our best sex was inspired spontaneity. On the couch. In the afternoon. In front of a flickering fire with *Scheherazade* playing. And other places and times that felt cinematic and electric and vaguely dangerous (even though we were married). Sometimes we held; sometimes we engaged in old-fashioned necking.

Remember? Now, even scheduled sex is no sure thing.


### Gee, It's Almost Trendy

Terri Hamilton, a certified sex therapist and professor in California, states, "The No. 1 sex problem facing couples today is they're not having sex." Hamilton says that "inhibited sexual desire," the clinical term for preferring sleep to lovemaking, will be a "very big issue in the nineties."

Some experts point to the rise in two-career

couples as dampening sexual relations between husbands and wives. These couples bring their briefcases to bed and turn in early to be ready for power breakfasts at seven the next morning.

This fixation on a relatively small percentage of the population overlooks the very real fatigue and busyness of the rest of us. Stay-at-home mothers of small children are worn out by nightfall. The husband working a blue-collar job comes home wanting nothing more than to crash in front of a video. Parents of older children often spend their evenings driving their kids places. No one is immune.

### Do You Think I'm Sexy?

Fatigue isn't the only enemy of sex. A deeper problem may be what my friend Carolyn pinpointed earlier: she struggles to think of herself as a "sexual being." We're conscientious parents, competent employees, companionable friends, faithful church-goers. We keep up our property, pay our taxes, floss daily. We're committed to our partners for the long haul and for the most part feel our marriages are in reasonable working order. But are we sexual, sensual creatures? Often the answer is, "Who, me?"

This may be more of an issue for women than for men. Several husbands interviewed have said they fancied marriage to be a continual sexual banquet. And even years into a settled marital relationship, the husband is likely to grab his wife (usually when she's in the midst of doing something romantic like bending over to clean out the garbage disposal) or admire the way she looks all dressed up for a night on the town.

The wife, on the other hand, feels fat, has her period, or just wants to fold laundry. And, as a wife named Joanne says, "For me, as a woman, thinking leads to doing. If my mind and heart aren't in it, the doing resembles a duty and is not too exciting."

Where does this come from? Children complicate sex in more ways than yelling out in the night. They can make you feel unsexy, sometimes for a long time. Psychotherapist JoAnn Magdoff says, "Nobody tells you how your deepest feelings are going to be changed and how the deepest connections with your mate will be altered. Your own sexuality will be altered once you have a child that has come of [that sexuality]." And sometimes, those altered feelings don't return for quite a while.

For women, another part of the sexual-being tension comes, I believe, from that old bugaboo, media influence. Sex is flaunted all over the airwaves—but, more critically, so is perfection. Hope Steadman on *thirtysomething*, for example, is supposed to be a harassed young mom who feels as if life and time are passing her by. The show is well written and well acted, so generally we empathize and believe—but whom do you know who looks like Mel Harris, the model-turned-actress who portrays Hope? Even with minimal makeup and hair stringing down, going to bed in a man's shirt, she looks fabulous—all tiny thighs and sculpted cheekbones. If *she* rarely has sex with her husband, and fantasizes about their bygone days of court and spark, what hope is there for the rest of us?

*Roseanne*, of course, is meant to show what Real Marriage is really like. True, Roseanne and Dan seem to really love each other; but who wants to be Roseanne, loud and sloppy and resigned? Television offers virtually no middle ground—where most of us live. So between rejecting Roseanne and envying Hope, most women continue to feel unsexy.

## So What?

Does it really matter? Readers are always writing to Ann Landers and "Dear Abby" saying things like, "My husband and I hardly ever have sex. But that's fine with me. We're content." Do we resign ourselves to a long dry season, knowing that in time the rains will come and our bodies will once again be joined? Quivering with cellulite and tattooed with spider veins, but joined nonetheless?

Of course it matters. Unsatisfactory or infrequent sex may push one partner into another's bedchamber. Or, to reverse Paul Newman's famous dictum, if you're getting only hamburger at home, going out for steak may cross your mind.

Not that one acts on the temptation. As Walter Wangerin observes, "He who takes seriously his declared commitment to the rose, the mutual relationship with his spouse, will guard the marriage even against the assaults of his own desires." But wait, there's more. A less-than-satisfactory sex life may open the door to mental infidelity—a much harder tiger to put back in the closet.

The fact is, those of us who regard the marriage vows as a sacred compact before God have even more of an obligation to nurture the sexual dimension of our relationship. This is for life; we are going to make it good.

We have all heard of saintly people whose spouses become permanently disabled with, say, Alzheimer's disease—and who still have remained faithful, affectionate partners, determined to uphold their end of the bargain even though it meant years and years of one-sided loving. We who have no such affliction need to take our commitment and build something bright and tapestried within its walls.

And one of the bright threads of that tapestry is a fulfilling life together as *man* and *woman*.

### Bind Us Together

Priest and novelist Andrew Greeley, author of a 1990 survey that shows adultery is actually less prevalent than has been thought, asserts that humans are not genetically encoded to be pair-bonded, like eagles or wolves. Rather, he says, we have been created with the capacity to attract and hold a partner of the opposite sex. Sexual life together is at the heart of this attractive capacity. Sex, says Greeley, "[holds] men and women together, [heals] the wounds created by the friction of the common life, and [renews] their love." Ironically, it is just that friction of the common life that comes between couples and sex— the friction sex is designed to heal.

We forget so fast. As a wife named Sandra says, "Sometimes we let a few weeks pass without sex, and I almost forget how good it can be. The longer we go without sex, the less I think about it. Then we almost force ourselves to make love, and when we're done, we both can't get over how great we feel. We find ourselves thinking, 'Why don't we do this more often?'"

Sex, then, matters deeply and wholly. *How much* sex is another question, however. One couple might be satisfied with monthly skyrockets. Another might prefer quantity over quality—thrice-weekly sparklers. But sometime, somewhere, somehow, you have to celebrate a rousing Fourth of July in a marriage. It's the way God intended man and woman to live together and, because sex is part of the design for partnership, it's a vital part of marriage.

A problem for many people is that there are no role models of good, clean sex. In a way that is as it should be too, for the sexual part of a relationship needs privacy in order to have intimacy. The kind of sex that is put on display is somehow dirty and degraded. Why can't there be sex that is at one and the same time deeply physical, highly erotic and yet honest, pure and clean?

I sometimes wonder if the people who look solemn and pious when they talk about the Bible have actually read it. The Song of Songs, those few consciously overlooked pages before the book of Isaiah, consists of joyful love poems that are intensely physical, evocative of tastes and perfumes, images and sensations that powerfully stir the emotions. The Bible's, and therefore God's, advice on marriage is not limited to vague terms like "love" and "respect," but includes a description of physical love rooted in earthiness yet thrilling to the heavens.

But don't forget the love and respect. Sometimes I feel that we've left the concept of duty far behind in sex as in too many other areas. Have we left it too far behind? Do we focus too much on the "feel-good" aspect of sex, on pleasing ourselves? In a marriage of mutual respect, a marriage where we strive to put our spouse's needs ahead of our own, should we engage in sex because it is important to the other, and therefore to us?

Certainly I am not suggesting the bad old ways of a husband brutalizing his passive wife. But as one wife interviewed said, "If my husband is in the mood, and we happen to have some time before bed, I may go along whether I feel like it or not, because he desires it so ardently. I've learned that he, too, craves emotional closeness and gentle touching—not just simple release. The thing is, I'll usually wind up enjoying it too."

Maybe the Roman candles go off; then again, maybe not. But we've made our spouse happy—and that, dear reader, is worth a lot.

---

## Making Your Marriage Sexy—In and Out of Bed

Are there ways to reclaim sexuality for its rightful turf—the marriage bed? How can we ease those frictions of common life that come between us and our partner? Here are a few thoughts.

◆ Think sexy. Someone has said that the brain is our primary sex organ. I don't know about that, but it is possible to cultivate a passionate, sensual, vulnerable, even humorous outlook on life—feelings that are components of great sex. Find a hobby that animates and energizes. Enjoy the subtle pleasures of cooking. Listen to music that moves you. Let yourself cry. Laugh out loud. Get back in touch with your emotions.

Dullness is the deadly enemy of sex. If we can keep ourselves interesting, alive, playful, informed, active—and yes, attractive—it's likely our sex lives will be all those things too.

◆ Be more physical. My husband and I have some of our sweetest times of closeness at the end of days when we've been out raking the yard or gone for a long hike. It's no accident that vacations tend to include great sex. There's something about moving your body, exploring nature, digging in dirt that awakens sexuality. Today, when so many of us work at white-collar desk jobs, we don't do these things often enough. Our brains are overtaxed; our bodies are undertaxed. Exercise and fresh air are relaxing—not tiring the way too much paper-shuffling is. When we are relaxed, rested, renewed, we become more open to sex.

◆ Remember that sex between the two of you does not stop at the bedroom door. Our interactions with our spouse can and should have a delightful undercurrent of sexiness—obviously not always, but often enough. From time to time, wearing something you know your mate especially likes is sexy.

Lengthy, lively conversations are sexy. Laughing together is *incredibly* sexy, particularly when it's a joke only the two of you get. Admiration of each other's bodies is sexy, even when, say, one of you is getting ready for a shower. And these are all things that can be done *before* the children are in bed.

◆ Work on exclusivity; create a "just-the-two-of-you" world. It's is often said that the old movies—Scarlett and Rhett go upstairs and close the door—were more erotic than today's explicit films because they could suggest more with a look than contemporary movies show with a nude scene. Sex is and should be an intensely private matter between two people. Locked doors are vital; behind them a husband and wife know privacy, intimacy and an unfolding of the mysteries of married love. Ideas, concerns, jokes, even silly names exclusive to a husband and wife signal something important: You are more important to me than anyone else—so important that some of these things between us do not go beyond the sacred oneness of our relationship.

◆ Worry less about sleep. Ah, sleep is a wonderful thing. I'm a devoted eight-hours-a-night person; I love snuggling down in flannel sheets in winter and pulling

74

up a heap of bedclothes, like an Eskimo sleeping under furs. In summer I love dozing off to the reassuring hum of the electric fan while a night wind comes through the open windows. But I've learned that sex can be the best sleep medicine there is—it's relaxing and sets the mood for a peaceful night.

Also, very few of us don't have an extra half-hour at the end of the day. It's a matter, sometimes, of giving something up. Maybe the nightly tidying doesn't get completely done. The news doesn't get watched; the paper goes unread. These corners of time are there for us: we need to be careful they don't get dusty.

Sometimes, of course, we truly need the rejuvenation that comes from late-evening solitude—reading a good book, for example. One young mother says she intentionally stays up late sometimes because it's the only time she has for herself. But we need to beware of *always* putting something else ahead of sex—ahead of our spouse.

◆ Don't scorn quickies. Many of us tend to think that sex has to be a wonderfully leisurely affair, with lots of tender preliminaries, the lights dimmed just so, a feeling of not being rushed. It's admittedly difficult to rapidly shift gears from "just tucked the kids in" to "ready for grand passion." Yet, just as sometimes a word of comfort or encouragement can speak volumes, so a brief time of physical intimacy can reaffirm love and commitment for your spouse—and excitement.

◆ Maximize those sudden moments of spark. The spontaneity issue is where many couples stumble. Planned sex seems so dull and dutiful, compared with being wildly swept away on a tide of passion. But there are moments we may capitalize on, however fleeting.

A particularly erotic hug or kiss can restart the electricity—and it can end there, if the time and place and circumstances are unpropitious.

◆ Remember the feelings. When we first fell in love with our spouses so many years ago, sexual attraction was a powerful reason why. We longed to be with them, to be touched by them. We wondered what it would be like, what they would look like. And the fact that somewhere along the line we decided to link our lives with theirs forever hallowed our sexual urges—made of them what Walter Wangerin calls "a clean joy." It felt right. It was right.

It still is. Our spouse hasn't changed *that* much— indeed, he or she probably has become deeper and more fascinating with age and experience and the things couples go through. They're still there for us.

## Chapter Six

# What If I'm Attracted to Someone Else?

*If anyone says they've never looked at
another person after marriage,
they're lying.*

Greg, married thirteen years

I've read dozens of articles and books, both by experts and victims, on the devastation adultery wreaks. But it was a television cartoon, of all things, that showed me how awful unfaithfulness can be.

*The Simpsons* is a satiric, animated look at a typical American family: dad Homer, who works in a nuclear power plant; mom Marge, a faithful churchgoer; and three kids. Homer has a perpetual five o'clock shadow; Marge's hair towers in an improbable beehive. The children are preternaturally wise. And the show is often hilarious. But one night it wasn't funny at all.

In the episode, Marge turns thirty-four and her husband gives her a bowling ball for her birthday—just what *he* would have wanted. Feeling disappointed and unloved, she goes by herself to try out her new ball at the local lanes, where she meets Jacques, the handsome resident bowling pro who attempts to teach her a lot more than the four-step delivery.

She finds herself becoming more and more drawn to Jacques. Meanwhile, back at the subdivision, poor mope Homer is sharing pizza with the kids and turning in early. On the second night Marge returns late from bowling, Homer, lying in the dark, says, "Marge?" "Yes?" she replies. Pause. "Nothing."

In the end Marge comes to a literal fork in the road where she has to decide between Homer and Jacques. In a cinematic finale, she chooses her husband. But for a few minutes there...

I slept fitfully that night. Images of Marge's ditzy need for romance and Homer's hurt, as simple as that of a rejected dog, flickered through my dreams, along with images of the children, who suspected something wrong. And Marge hadn't technically done anything wrong. Yet, it was close enough.

## "If She, Why Not Me?"
Why did a cartoon show stick with me? I think it was because the Simpsons are so unremarkable. Marge, no beauty, is a patient wife. And hard-working Homer, though at times gruff, is really a good guy. Ordinary folks all around. And the question comes: "If she, why not me?" or "If he could, I could." It's enough to make you shiver and cling to your spouse a little tighter.

Gordon MacDonald was a rising star among religious leaders when his career came to an abrupt halt several years ago after he confessed to an affair. MacDonald had everything; he seemed the model of the successful comer. He had taken the reins of a national campus ministry, following a lengthy tenure as pastor of a New England church. His books regularly made the religious best-seller lists. He was an engaging and thoughtful speaker, in demand for conferences. He and his wife, Gail, lectured frequently on marriage. It all ended when he made his confession.

*Why would he do it?* He had been weary, MacDonald said. His judgment was clouded. He resigned his position, and he and Gail went into seclusion in New Hampshire to think and pray and receive help from trusted friends.

He writes: "For the rest of my life I will have to live with the knowledge that I brought deep sorrow to my wife, to my children, and to friends and others who have trusted me for many years."

That's painful. We hear it so often—"No one is immune"—that we can become dull to the warning. Gordon's story is cautionary. But, again, *if he could...*

I begin this chapter with the bad news because I want to respond to the "attraction" question with a warning: if you are attracted to someone else, this is what that feeling may lead to. Know that the danger is always there.

## The Starting Point

I'm always amazed at how the Bible *makes sense*. Take the commandmant, "thou shalt not commit adultery." Why did God see fit to include it in his instructions to the people of Israel—and us? Obviously God thought preserving the sanctity of the marriage covenant was important enough to be included with his other overarching rules: Don't kill. Don't steal. Keep the Sabbath. Worship no other gods before me.

Today, when it seems so many good people are

falling, so many marriages shattering, the commandment makes bright and shining sense. Adultery can kill marriages. Many counselors say that when trust has been broken, it's never fully restored. There's always that shadow of doubt. The marriage may survive—but something has been irretrievably lost. Sanctity has been profaned.

God is not some celestial prison warden, locking us away from sunshine. He created marriage, he wants our marriages to thrive. He knows that when a union is exclusive—one man, one woman, for life—it can bring the deepest tenderness and joy.

Mary Roxburgh put it this way: "I guess ours was the era when absolute standards went out the window, when you decided what was right for you and didn't lay down the law for other people. The Ten Commandments, and the one about 'thou shalt not commit adultery,' were too rigid. Okay, I might decide that for myself, but could it be true for everyone?

"It wasn't till I had kids that I realized that absolute rules have a place. I remember taking my three under-fives along a busy street. I had to keep them away from the edge of the sidewalk. It had to be a rule: don't walk along the edge of the sidewalk. The risks, the consequences, were just too awful. One sensible rule to keep their lives safe, to be obeyed absolutely. And God's rule to keep a marriage safe."

### And yet...

We may know all this intellectually. We abhor the idea of a clandestine fling. And the majority of American married couples—according to recent data—*are* faithful. But here is the truth: One of the best-kept secrets couples have is the fact that some—many?—of us may be attracted to another. It may be a fleeting blink of a feeling, or the attraction may be more long-term. We may be drawn to an interesting stranger, but it is more likely the object of our interest will be someone we already know.

We may not do anything about it. We may peek out the window and then close it, no harm done. We may form a close friendship and leave it at that. Or we may fall into something much darker.

Where is the line of danger—in thought or deed? Is a mild flirtation healthy? Is it all right to silently look and admire? Does everyone do it? What's wrong with treating the opposite sex as the opposite sex? Where are the minefields of cross-sex friendships?

These questions are not as naive as they sound. It's easy, in the nineties, to shrug all this off. After all, we're adults. Men and women work together in offices every day; there's a huge gulf between flirting and unfaithfulness.

Is there?

## Just Looking, Thanks

I have always enjoyed men, and have always been aware they were something *other* than what I am. The creation of the two sexes ranks right up there with rainbows and singing whales as one of God's great ideas. And awareness of sexual differences is a country mile from infidelity. After all, we certainly looked at our spouses—and noticed they were different from us—before we became seriously involved. In a marriage where passion is alive, we continue to notice and celebrate those differences.

Yet that awareness, when it comes to those outside our marriage, must be carefully applied. The fact is, we're going to look. We were made that way. The gray area comes when we step from looking into *thinking*—into admiring, wondering, comparing.

Radio personality David Mains, who has been married for more than twenty years, speaks of the "careful channeling of all your romantic feelings to one person alone—your marriage partner. Comparisons...are to exist no more... The moment such thoughts appear, refuse to entertain them."

Easy to say, harder to do? Yes. Certainly comparisons are wrong and can be destructive. The fact is, though, that some of these feelings are driven less by an attraction to a specific person than by a restlessness in our own lives, a wistful longing to recapture the way we felt at twenty, or the way we felt during our courtship.

Most of us hope that every time will be like the first. We *know* ours will be the grand passion that prevails against time and gum disease and daily dreariness. Our marriage is different.

Then we discover our marriage is not different. But we remember the edge, the mystery, of beginning love—be that love painful or abiding joy. When I was in college, I was powerfully drawn to a drama student named Peter. High cheekbones, classic nose, curly auburn hair. I couldn't resist. The experience was wonderful, painful, altogether poignant. At twenty you love feeling that way.

Five years later, I met another guy and I felt the same way. I would look up his number in the phone book and stare at it. I would write frightful romantic verse in my journal. I wondered if he would call—and he did.

He kept calling, and we dated, and he's now my husband. I know him inside and out; I've seen him cut his toenails and weep for his dead father. He takes the covers at night and brings me coffee in bed in the morning. Most of all, this I know: he will always be there for me.

82

Most of us treasure this assurance, the security of living with the one we love. But at times we all miss the edge of courtship. All the advice about "dating your mate" overlooks the central point: Courtship is surprise. There's magic in the unknown; it's the stuff of fantasy. Unless your spouse goes on your date night in disguise, even the most intimate restaurant-booth-for-two setting won't recapture the early feelings.

We *know* what our wife or husband thinks of us. We know what they look like when they're home sick with stomach flu. That's marvelous and comforting. But we all have a basic need for surprise, for discovery. The richest marriages I know are those where the partners say, "She keeps surprising me, keeps growing. After fifteen years I'm still finding out things about this woman." Or, "He continues to develop new interests, to reveal unsuspected depths. He's much bigger than the man I married."

The combination of security and surprise is well-nigh irresistible in a marriage. It sure beats pining in the dorm room. And it keeps the feelings where they belong.


## How Close Is Too Close?

"In most of us the connections among attraction, affection, sexuality and love are complicated and not always conscious," observe Evelyn and James Whitehead. Today we are surrounded by possibilities for cross-sex friendship: in the office, through church and civic work, via couple-to-couple friendships. A wise friend of mine, Christine, observes, "Opposite-sex friendships are no longer a matter of choice. They're there."

But are they dangerous? Not necessarily,

according to the Whiteheads, who contend that our culture's emphasis on sexuality—the notion that any connection between male and female must have an erotic component—is wrong and possibly danger-ous, in that exaggerated caution may backfire into self-fulfilling prophecy.

The least healthy thing we can do is isolate ourselves, grade-school style, with our own sex: No Girls Allowed! Boys Keep Out!—with the sole exception being our mate. My husband and I have work friends, church friends, college friends of both sexes. Healthy, lively interaction with the opposite sex helps us understand one another, helps us tolerate the sometimes amusing, sometimes irritating differences between the sexes: "I was talking with Brian about a concern and I could tell he wasn't listening. Now I tell you and *you* aren't listening. Why are men like that?" Because my husband is also friends with Brian, he too can be amused at the similarity—and try to explain "why men are like that."

That's the key: my husband is also friends with Brian. Because while we ought not to assume a cross-sex friendship will become something else, we also ought not to assume it won't. Deep friendship and delightful compatibility can very easily slide into the territory of an emotional affair—an intimate and exclusive friendship that may not be sexual, but is unfaithful in that we are developing a heavy emotional involvement with someone who is not our spouse. There are many kinds of betrayals. And such betrayals are certain to ruin a promising friendship.

Rich, rewarding friendships are difficult to find and harder to hold on to. And as we become more established in our careers, as our children need less constant attention, friends start to matter more, become more cherishable.

On the other hand, illicit affairs are all too easy to find—if we look hard enough. Especially in the workplace.

Today, of course, many of our closest friendships spring up in the workplace. It's where many of us spend most of our time; it's where we look our best; it's where we are working with people of like interests, ambitions, aspirations. The office is also the place where excitement and shared projects and common interests can fuse into something potent. The office can be a place of great sexual tension.

American society has devised all sorts of elaborate behaviors to cope with this tension. First, we don't touch much, and when we do—even the tiniest brush of shoulder or arm—we exclaim, "Whoops! Excuse me!" There are excellent reasons for this.

At a company I once worked for, two employees in another department worked closely for months on an accounting project, trying to straighten out the books of one division. They put in long days and late nights. Both were married. But the emotional intimacy sparked by the closeness flared into an affair, and they resigned in disgrace.

### Drawing the Boundaries

Suzanne Hague is an executive on the West Coast. She is an attractive woman with a dry wit and a couple of advanced degrees, and she works closely with a number of men.

Suzanne states: "You can have incredible intellectual, emotional and spiritual friendships—but you have to define the boundaries."

Suzanne has come across a number of successful men who married their high-school sweethearts, raised families, prospered professionally, became pillars in their churches—and grew beyond their wives. Now, she says, they're engaged in "emotional affairs" with younger women in the office. These couples confide in each other, meet each other's emotional needs (or think they do), and keep the relationships somewhat secret. No sex, but, says Suzanne, plenty of infidelity.

As I interviewed people about healthy and unhealthy friendships, the phrases *set limits* or *define the boundaries* came up often. Not everyone, however, agrees on how to draw those boundaries. Several men I know say they make it a rule never to lunch alone with a woman they're not related to; others dismiss that as moralistic paranoia.

Knowing yourself is vital. Are you like the alcoholic who has to stay away from strong temptation? Or can you handle healthy interaction with the opposite sex? Are you especially vulnerable because of stress at work or at home? Are you worldly-wise enough to recognize a come-on when you see one? Do you know how to say no, even to a direct question?

---

## What Is Acceptable?

Many of us do—or will—find ourselves in potentially compromising situations from time to time. However, completely avoiding such situations (a business trip, for example) may not be realistic. And as we have seen, outside friendships and involvements have a salutary effect on a marriage.

Yet the majority of affairs happen among friends. How do

we ensure that a healthy friendship doesn't escalate into something destructive?

Peter Kreitler says, "I have found that it is not enough for couples to simply affirm a belief in fidelity on their wedding day and then presume that 'in-loveness' will carry them through to eternity." Kreitler advises that couples discuss what is acceptable and what is not. Couples need to talk out such issues as:

◆ Acceptable office behavior. Is lunch with an opposite-sex colleague okay, but dinner off-limits? What about being alone after hours with him or her, working on a project? If business travel is necessary, do the rules change?

◆ Socializing. It's quite common for one spouse to be a more enthusiastic party-goer than the other, who will stand in the corner and look glum unless someone rescues him. But this poses problems. Can the more extroverted partner carry on a long conversation with an attractive man? Is it all right for the husband to dance with an old family friend?

◆ Separate interests. Can one spouse go to a party alone? Play mixed doubles without his mate? See a movie with a friend?

Many marriages have foundered on the rocks of faulty assumptions. Don't let yours be one of them!

## Windows and Locks
Yes. We notice. We may daily interact with delightful, stimulating and attractive members of the opposite sex. We may have same-sex friends who meet all kinds of emotional and intellectual needs.

But if the outside world is too much with us—even in innocent encounters—we risk marital inattention, indifference, lost intimacy. Most of all, we risk losing the *primacy* of our marriage—the special, central place it should occupy in our minds, hearts and spirits.

I'm writing this at the desk in our bedroom. It's a Saturday afternoon, spring. I can look out a large window, framed with frilly curtains, facing the street. I love windows; I cannot work without them. Through the window grass greens, robins feed, scilla peeps above the earth. Cars run the YIELD sign on our corner. The sun disappears, a neighbor passes.

I need my window.

But it's cold outside today. Inside, the furnace kicks on. I can hear my daughter in the living room, talking to herself and building an empire with wooden blocks. The laundry is going around in the basement. Gentle waves of plainsong come from the stereo. The doors are shut tight against the wind.

My husband is here. I hear him moving about, doing chores. I'm contented. No one else is here. Nor should they be.

I don't want my marriage to be an airless room with curtains drawn, deadbolted against the world with the only light artificial. I need the sky and storm and sunshine. I don't even mind if it rains in: I prefer open windows to air conditioning.

But I also need snugness. Not for me the open plan of a city loft or contemporary home with great glassy rooms. No: I need to be able to close doors, draw drapes, turn my back on the passersby.

*Because* I have my view out the window, because I can have the breeze blowing in and the courting call of the cardinal ringing in the tree, I can turn away from the outside world and turn to my hearth, my husband.

We can, together, look out.

---

## How to Keep a Beautiful Friendship from Being Ruined

◆ Be aware of the type of person you find especially attractive—and act accordingly. The same rules don't govern a friendship with the elderly widow next door and a friendship with the arty-looking wife of your best friend—especially if you're drawn to artistic types (or athletes, or intellectuals, or whatever).

◆ Be careful of spending too much time alone with a member of the opposite sex. A corollary applies here, especially where office friendships are concerned: watch appearances.

◆ Watch out for vulnerable days. Everyone has them, the days when we feel we've lost our last friend, we're fat, we're failures, our marriage is stagnant, our career is stalled. The consolation of a listening ear can too easily turn into a reassuring hug. Tell your troubles to your mother.

◆ Remember that touch is powerful. Watch how, when and especially whom you touch.

◆ Relearn to appreciate your spouse as a sexual being. Many affairs, even mild flirtations, arise out of sexual boredom. Being physical with your mate, seeing him or her as a hunk or love goddess, will go far to prevent the roving eye and hand.

◆ Say no. Psychological considerations aside, it's in the

Ten Commandments: "Thou shalt not commit adultery." Every once in a while we need to respond to the "Why not?" question with a stern "Because it's *wrong.*"

## Chapter Seven

# How Much Do I Have to Put Up With?

*So often, what's important to you*
*is not important to me,*
*and vice versa.*
*It's the natural trap*
*of two persons living together.*

Harold Myra

This is how my husband gets up:

Put on robe and slippers. Close door on sleeping wife. Wash. Turn on garish overhead fluorescent light in kitchen. Put tape in stereo—music or "mood" tape. Make coffee in energy-hogging modern coffee maker. Spill coffee while pouring. Neglect to wipe. Leave dish drainer overflowing from the night before. Fetch newspaper. Remove plastic cover. Throw cover on floor. Open drapes but leave them askew. Turn on too many lights in living room.

He, of course, sees his morning routine as quiet, orderly, enjoyable—and mine as different, not the way *he* would do it. When I get up first, I turn on news radio, which he thinks is intrusive chatter; leave lights off, which he thinks is living in gloom; empty the dish drainer, which he thinks is compulsive.

We don't do well getting up at the same time. Our habits bump into one another.

Everyone has habits; everyone has opinions on them. Advice columnist Ann Landers received something like fifty thousand letters on the right way to unroll toilet paper. Habits—repeat behaviors so ingrained we may not even realize we are doing them—can be a source of affectionate amusement, fleeting pique or grinding irritation. Some can be changed; some should be changed; some are not worth bickering about.

No one ever left a spouse simply over the annoying way she starts every sentence with "Well..." or his maddening habit of fiddling with buttons on the dashboard before turning on the ignition. Some habits, because they are like ours, we feel comfortable with. But if too many molehills of annoyance pile up, they can form a respectable pile of dirt, until one day we realize: This person really bugs me.

### Swat!
I call these annoying habits the mosquitoes of marriage. They're tiny, they're infuriating, they're persistent, and they can draw blood. Some are relatively harmless. Others, however, can carry deadly disease. They can ruin your marital picnic. And they flourish under certain climatic conditions.

Some of us are more bothered by mosquitoes than others. My husband and I are veterans of many church and clergy retreats, usually held in July at some church camp where the mosquitoes are as big as chickadees and a lot meaner. No one ever seems to have sprayed. Mosquitoes tend to bite me, so I would be itchy and mumbling and miserable, while others at the retreat would airily wave the mosquitoes away and *laugh* about the situation.

Things get under my skin. I can't look at a crooked picture; I have to straighten it. If I see a child with a dirty mouth, I want to wipe it. Mosquitoes annoy me.

And yet I, too, produce my share.

It's easy to use terms like lovable, quirky, eccentric. It's easy to say "accept each other's differences." It's easy to say "overlook the bad and embrace the good." It's a lot harder to put into practice.

### In the White Room

Lori and Hal Williams live in a spotless contemporary house. The walls are white, the windows wide, giving onto a wooded ravine. Their large glass coffee table is pristine, free of water rings or finger marks (even though they have two active children). The kitchen, Eurostyle black and white, could be used as a place to perform minor surgery.

Lori, active and fit, thinks she is compulsive. She now works part-time, but it is still difficult for her to relax her standards. Hal, while no slob, is more easygoing.

"Hal free floats," Lori says. Her motto is, "If you get these things done, then they'll be *done* and we won't have to worry about them." Translation: "*I* won't have to worry about them." Because, as Lori admits, "I get so I literally can't stand looking at things like the laundry piled up. It's a visual offense."

She has fought against this tendency, but with little success to date. She reflects, "I know I can be like a slave driver. So the general family consensus is

'Let's just do it and keep Mom happy.' There's a saying that goes something like this: 'If Mama ain't happy, ain't *nobody* happy.'

"But the reverse is never true, interestingly; I can never ignore things to make Hal happy."

It irritates Lori when Hal stacks the dishes without loading them in the dishwasher. It annoys Hal when Lori does not "tear here" when opening a package. Lori, more quick-tempered, is bugged by Hal's habit of arguing in a logical, dispassionate, lawyerly style. Hal escapes to the garage when Lori, as he puts it, "indulges herself by yelling."

All these things are habits—of household maintenance, speech patterns, communication. But because Hal and Lori tend to agree on the important matters—goals and values and children—they live with the mosquitoes. They don't like them, and they swat them a lot, but they live with them.

### Beyond the Toilet-Paper Roll

Habits go beyond the toilet-paper roll. A habit is an unexamined pattern of behavior, something we do over and over. We may bring these patterns to marriage from our childhood, or we may develop them in the early years of our relationship—for good or for ill. Crabbiness can become a habit. So can rudeness or critical carping. "We talk to our spouses in ways we would never talk to someone else," observes Harold Myra. We use "the tone of voice that demeans, that says, 'Hey, you jerk, aren't you done yet?'... The tone of voice between spouses is too often less respectful than the tone toward someone else."

Moodiness can be a very big, very painful mosquito. Kay Jansen and her husband, Dick, don't argue about refrigerating the butter or picking

94

up his socks. But Dick is subject to low moods, times when he comes home testy and touch-me-not. "I used to try to get him out of it," says Kay. "He didn't want me to. Now if *I'm* feeling down, I want someone to ask me what's wrong, to try to talk about it. He just wants to be left alone. I finally decided: if he's having a bad day, why should I have a bad day? Now I've learned to leave him alone, and he comes out of it faster." Kay has found a partial solution to something that has been a puzzling, painful habit for all fourteen years of their marriage.

Nagging plagues many marriages. Charlene Ann Baumbich, who calls herself "Queen Snipe" for indulging in a sharp-edged tone with her husband, writes that the longer a couple has been married, the more entrenched nagging can become a habit. We feel secure in our marriages, so we don't worry about the effect our bad habits might have on our spouse. We take our spouse for granted.

## Partners in Crime

Occasionally couples can reinforce one another's bad habits—overeating, watching too much television, overspending, general messiness. I have one friend, Dorothy, who admits: "Frank and I are both slobs, in a way. I don't like it, but it's one less thing for us to fight about."

Another wife, Becky Richter, observed, "My husband and I are a lot alike. Maybe too much alike. I've always thought that if a couple are *too* different in personality it makes their marriage really hard. I saw that in my parents, who are very different; it seemed like every decision, everything they did entailed huge negotiations, misunderstandings and sometimes outright conflict. They're still married after many years, but it's been tough every step of the way.

"Now I see, though, that similarity can be a mixed blessing, especially when it comes to reinforcing the bad habits. It's taken me eleven years to find that out. For example, Tom and I both tend to be somewhat introverted. We're homebodies—he is more than I am, but to avoid conflict I'll just go along. If we're invited somewhere, he'll say, 'Oh, let's not go out tonight.' I'll say something like, 'Yeah, I'm tired and it's probably going to snow.' It isn't healthy; you need more of that 'iron sharpens iron' that the Bible talks about."

One of the beauties of a good marriage is the prodding, loving accountability of spouse to spouse. Differences can stir up the pot, keep life interesting. Couples who are too much alike can sink into a complacent semi-doze of a relationship. Healthy marriages are relationships in which each partner balances out the other's less desirable habits, by both example and direct encouragement.

### Why the Serenity Prayer Isn't a Cliché
There is no consensus among experts regarding the possibilities for change in a partner. "Don't think he'll change once you're married!" Mom warns her starry-eyed daughter. And, left to their own devices, people can be lazy, selfish, resistant even to positive change that would benefit a marriage.

Yet this is where the much-abused phrase "born again" springs to life. When Jesus and a man named Nicodemus met for a private chat, and Jesus told the worthy Jewish leader that he had to be "born again," he wasn't offering him membership in some exclusive Christian club. He was talking about the need to acknowledge our dark side—and open ourselves to God's transforming love. Even when we're dealing with marriage's mosquitoes.

This kind of transformation goes far beyond the latest formula for weight loss or positive thinking. It's about letting the whole basis of our lives be changed, along with our motivations, aims and goals.

How does this work itself out in practical terms, in the daily rubbing-up-against-each-other that is marriage? After all, being a Christian does not automatically erase all irritating habits. However, it *does* mean we become more aware of our shortcomings, and actually *want* to erase them. And marriage, a strong marriage, provides a secure background in which both husband and wife can let this fundamental change affect all they do, right down to the seemingly trivial issues.

I like the approach taken by William Willimon, chaplain at Duke University and a prominent United Methodist author and speaker: "One of the best ways to change me," he said in a recent interview, "is to first of all truly love me. Truly accept me.... I think that's why people can say, after twenty years of marriage, 'I know this woman has made me a better person.'"

Change, says Willimon, is the fruit of marriage. He cited a survey of married men, who, when asked what marriage meant to them, responded: "This woman has shown me parts of my personality I didn't know were there." So, although you imagine you are changing, marriage is actually helping you become *more* like yourself—more like the self God intended you to be.

Becky Richter can attest to this: "Tom often told me he never used to consider himself a particularly funny person—until he met me and we spent some time together. Now he's quick, witty, even silly. I think he always had a sense of humor, but somehow I brought it out."

And, of course, it's virtually impossible to live with someone day in and day out and not adjust your stride to his. It's the old idea of spouses growing to resemble each other more and more as the years go by. I catch myself thinking like my husband, using some of the same little quirks of speech, worrying about some of the same things. And I know he's picked up some things from me, too—everything from wiping the stove to a certain crisp assertiveness.

Mutual respect and deep cherishing in a marriage relationship mean that we care enough to learn what is truly important to our partner. If it means changing an annoying habit, so be it.

We've all seen the Serenity Prayer on dozens of plaques, posters, bookmarks, counted cross-stitch samplers, and on and on: "God grant me the serenity to accept the things I cannot change; courage to change the things I can, and wisdom to know the difference." Theologian Reinhold Niebuhr's prayer may be overfamiliar, but it contains a reminder crucial for married couples: give us the wisdom to know the difference between the things we can change and the things we simply have to accept.

For example, every night I go through a bedtime ritual that grates on my husband like fingernails on a chalkboard. It makes my morning preparations look downright catch-as-catch-can. My husband can brush his teeth and jump into bed and he's ready for the night. Whereas I, with infinite, painstaking slowness and precision, observe an elaborate rite: Pick up the house, very deliberately. Check to see if the doors are locked. Ask him if the doors are locked. Come into the bedroom. Slowly hang up clothes or put them in hamper. Dress for bed. (The other night, my husband looked at me and said, "Do you realize you stand in exactly the same place every night when you get ready for bed?" Well, we have a small bedroom. But still.) Tuck in a tip of sock hanging out of his drawer (Touché! One of *his* habits.). Place slippers under the chair, just so. Disappear into the bathroom for lengthy evening ablutions. Peer at crow's feet. Hang up an errant towel.

Eventually I get to bed. Sometimes my husband will be awake and reading; other times he will have given up and be fast asleep. I know all these elaborate preparations bother him; I also know that they are probably psychologically and possibly even physiologically necessary to assure peaceful sleep for me. My mother tells me that I was a child who embraced deliberate ritual and, indeed, was unsettled by disruptions in familiar patterns. I was that way at four. I'm not likely to change at forty.

This is where micro-changes within the context of macro-patterns might be called for. My ritual is not really harmful, not like a bad mood or sniping tone of voice might be. Still, it bothers my husband, because he'd like to get to bed a little earlier. So I'm working on backing everything up fifteen minutes or so. Without cutting anything out of my evening ritual. Not quite succeeding yet...but aware of the problem. And trying. Sometimes, that's all we can do.

And my husband is working on his sense of humor about all this.

### The Joy of Routines

There's a little secret to habits and rituals and routines: some of them make us happy. They provide safety, security, predictability. And when we, with our spouses, create new and fairly healthy routines, the satisfaction can verge on joy.

I have heard celebrities say they wish they could do

STRONG MARRIAGES, SECRET QUESTIONS

more "normal-person" things like walking the dog, mailing a letter, scrubbing the bathroom. It doesn't surprise me. There's a sweet solace in homeliness (in the better, British sense of the term), a comfort in the anticipated rhythms of daily activities. I may, and do, grouse about the plastic newspaper wrap on the carpet. But I love it that my husband is out there reading. I know what we'll say in the morning; I know he'll ask plaintively, "What's for breakfast?" And I know I will gently tease him about asking it.

Sure, the word *rut* hides in the word *routine*. That's always a danger, and it's something we're working on (he surprised me with breakfast in bed this morning). New, shared experiences infuse a marriage with the fresh blood of excitement.

But the pleasures of homeliness—what we might call the sacrament of the plain, because it points to God's quiet gifts—is the underpinning of life together. I pity couples who miss out on this, who escape into constant travel, exhausting work, or the drug of too much manufactured entertain ment. They miss out on so much, including each other.

And that sweetness, that ordinariness has much to do with the dozens of habits that help to weave our personalities. I've learned to see that some of my husband's most annoying habits are simply the flip side of some of his most endearing traits. He doesn't empty the dish drainer in the morning because he's taking time to pray—or bring me coffee in bed.

Even the mess of the newspaper wrap is endearing, in a way, because it's him. When I made my vows at the altar, I didn't commit to only part of him. I accepted the entire package—including the mosquitoes that sometimes plague our picnic.

STRONG MARRIAGES, SECRET QUESTIONS

## Ladybugs, Not Mosquitoes

Not all habits are bad. Courtesy can become a habit; so can kindness. Even kissing one's mate when leaving the house for the day can become a habit, and a good one (though, as a recent survey shows, only two-thirds of couples aged thirty-five to forty-four keep it up).

"Habits weave the very fabric of our relationship," observes Scott Bolinder. "I make the bed; Jill gets up to have breakfast with me; we drink coffee (decaf now) and talk each night after the moppets are in bed. These *good* habits make each of us feel affirmed and appreciated." By contrast, he notes, bad habits can make partners feel taken for granted and uncared-for.

Habits don't have to be like irksome mosquitoes. They can be more like the helpful ladybugs who eat nasty pests in our gardens and ensure that our plants thrive. The ladybugs are every bit as persistent as the mosquitoes. We don't hear them; ladybugs are silent. We don't often see them. But most of us, when we find a ladybug who has accidentally wandered into our house, will gently pick her up (ladybugs are always "she") and take her outdoors, to fly away and find some destructive aphid to eat.

The nasty or merely annoying habits may not go away. They may, like mosquitoes (which are found practically everywhere in the world except Antarctica), be an inescapable fact of life and marriage. But we need not give up and simply allow ourselves to get bitten to the point of near-madness. We need not shrug and say, Take me or leave me, nasty habits and all. We *can* patch screens so that mosquitoes don't come in our house. We can apply repellent; we can rid our yards of stagnant water where mosquitoes breed.

So too we can rid our marriages of the stagnant pools of complacency and laziness and taking-for-granted that foster the growth of bad and destructive habits. And—as always—we can be mindful of what's important to the other. And—of course—we can laugh and swat. For sometimes that is the only response.

Likewise, we can, and should, care for the lady-bugs in our gardens. When we find one lying helpless on her back, waving her legs, we can tenderly right her. We can plant our gardens to attract the little creatures. We can nurture and encourage the ladybugs of positive, helpful habits in our marriages; recognize those things that build closeness and trust; cherish the sweetness of routine.

It may take much awareness and effort (Scott Bolinder has to consciously think about making the bed every morning). The ladybug, for her part, doesn't have to think about what she's doing. She simply goes about her business as the Creator intended.

But so, in a way, do we.

---

### It's Habit-Forming...and Good for You!

My daughter has a child's bank with the inscription "Little and often fills the purse" written on it. So it is in marriage. The good little things we put into it add up to a marriage rich in enjoyment and mutual understanding.

You may not be able to break your spouse of every annoying habit, but you *can* help each other to form good habits, which may offset the bad ones. Here are a few tips:

◆ Build up and affirm your mate. If your spouse surprises you by cleaning up the kitchen after dinner, express gratitude; don't just dismiss it as something he should do anyway. After we've been married a few years we tend to dismiss the good things our spouse does. Don't fall into that trap.

◆ Enlist your spouse's help in developing good habits (and eliminating the bad ones). If one of you is struggling with a weight problem, for example, avoid the nagging/defensiveness cycle. Say honestly to your husband or wife, "I really want to lose weight. Could you help me by encouraging me—not policing me?" Give some specific ideas.

◆ Stop carping about the other's bad habits. It's a perverse fact of human nature that the more we are nagged at and criticized, the worse the behavior that prompted the criticism becomes. Often, silence is the best response. Sometimes when you ignore something, it really does go away.

◆ Accept those things that are simply different and probably harmless. A lark, for example, is *not* superior to an owl. Morning people are not morally superior to night people. They're just different. Agree to disagree, and move on from there.

◆ Establish a habit by repeating a good behavior. It is said that if you do anything—jogging, getting eight hours' sleep a night, eating right—for ten days, it will become a habit, incorporated into your life. Try consciously to do something repeatedly. Go for ten days without complaining about the bills, for instance.

◆ Pray with your spouse about these habits. Seek God's assistance in dealing with them (not a bad habit to form in itself).

## Chapter Eight

# Do We Have to Be Together All the Time?

*It is the separateness of partners that enriches the union.*

M. Scott Peck

Morning, about 5:30. The head of our queen-sized bed is right up under the window. In summertime it feels as if we're sleeping outdoors. I like the way the light peeps in under the shade, a gentle reveille.

But I'm not ready to get up. I bunch the pillows under my head, roll on my side—and hope my husband awakens soon. I want to be alone in bed for my last hour or so of sleep. I wish he'd go. I love spread-eagling over the bed, taking all the covers I want, dozing away in solitary splendor.

*Go away. I want to be alone.* I feel guilty.

In their study of long-term married couples, *'Til Death Do Us Part,* Jeanette and Robert Lauer agree, saying that such couples have established "zones of freedom within a shared relationship.... Togetherness is very important to them, but they recognize

that it is two different people who are together."
Happy couples are not Siamese twins.

How, then, should we be together in marriage?
How do we give each other space without that space
becoming a gulf that separates?

## Do Moles Have the Right Idea?
The Langleys have been married twenty-four years.
Austin is CEO of a fast-growing high-technology
firm. Maureen, a former teacher, opens her home to
troubled teenagers needing a listening ear, a good
meal and a place to stay for a while. The Langleys
have two teens of their own.

Austin is a brilliant conceptual thinker and a
powerful, intense—some would say driven—
personality. Maureen is a warm, energetic woman
with an appealing little-girl quality. She thrives on
people; Austin does not. He is organized to the point
of compulsion; Maureen is more spontaneous, less
systematic.

Maureen wants to be affirmed; Austin wants to be
alone. Both needs have to do with giving the partner
physical and emotional breathing space. The Langleys do enjoy each other's company; they just have
different needs for it. "Maureen would say that I
disappear into the den for hours at a time," Austin
said. Meanwhile, Maureen is opening the door to
another teenager.

Recently, Austin compared the difficulties of men
and women living together day to day with, of all
things, moles. "They burrow along, all by themselves. Then once a year, only once, the male comes
to the female. They mate—and that's it."

## The Delicate Dance
The Langleys, like many couples who have been

married awhile, are engaged in a delicate pas de deux of solitude versus companionship. Fortunately, both are aware of their "optimum range of togetherness," in the words of counselors Evelyn and James Whitehead. At any given point in a marriage relationship, "there is likely to be a balance of being together and being alone that works best for us. Some couples seem able to sense the rhythm of privacy and togetherness that works best for them; others may need to work out explicit patterns of physical and emotional separateness."

Kris and Dave Parrish have been married twenty years. Dave is a school principal; Kris works part-time in an antiques shop. Like the Langleys, they have three teenagers. Unlike the Langleys, the Parrishes have similar needs for solitude. They have found the right "rhythm of privacy and togetherness."

Part of this is due to their similar temperaments. Both are shy. "We're not Mr. and Mrs. Magnetic Personality," Kris admits. When they have free time, they like to be home—sometimes together, sometimes separately. For them, marriage "in the forties" is great and getting better. They've learned to give each other more breathing room.

"We've lengthened the rope," Kris explains. "We've gotten some freedom from having to do everything together as a couple. I'm a separate person from Dave."

Recently Dave spent three months in Ecuador, where he was born. He climbed mountains, visited native villages, returned to the haunts of his youth. Kris and the girls did not accompany him. "Lots of people have made jokes like, 'Oh, leaving the wife and kids behind, huh?' They don't understand how we could do it. But we're comfortable being apart."

During their separation, Dave phoned Kris every week at a prearranged time. And, while Kris didn't mind the time apart, she admits she was overjoyed when her husband returned—at which time they immediately took off for a family vacation.

## Donna Reed's Bed

In *The Donna Reed Show,* a popular television sitcom of the early sixties, Donna and Alex Stone were shown talking in their bedroom, sitting up in twin beds with quilted headboards. Ten years later John and Olivia Walton, characters on *The Waltons,* snuggled in a double bed, falling asleep in each other's arms. Ten years after that, Cliff and Claire Huxtable from *The Cosby Show* nuzzled and sighed in a king-sized bed. We knew what *they* were going to do.

Married sex portrayed on TV—isn't that refreshing? Yet many couples cannot imagine falling asleep in each other's arms. They try it once or twice and wind up sweaty and uncomfortable. Paul and Ruth Giddings have had similar bedtime blues. The Giddingses married at nineteen. "Their" song was the then-popular "I Think We're Alone Now." Twenty-two years later their idea of marital compatibility is the freedom to get a good night's sleep in the spaciousness of a new king-sized bed. "I can extend my long legs and he can twitch and kick, and we can still wake up friends," Ruth says. "Our sex life is fine; it's the literal *sleeping together* that's the problem!"

Many couples will affirm that the invention of large beds has saved many a marriage. By contrast, a double bed contains about the same space for each adult occupant as a baby's crib. I have known couples who started out in beautiful heirloom double beds, only to switch to twin beds in their middle years. Now I can see the reasoning. Maybe Donna Reed and her doctor-husband had a point after all.

I am grateful that my husband is a relatively quiet sleeper, as am I. And I am comforted by the gentle whoosh of his regular breathing, the solid closeness of his pajamas-clad bulk. But I want him to stay on his side of the bed. Not touching. There, but not touching.

## Total Togetherness?

In recent years, those of us with strong religious commitments have heard much about preserving the family. Preachers have inveighed against the looking-out-for-number-one mentality, an over-emphasis on self at the expense of others. Many Christians, in fact, learned the acronym "JOY" in Sunday school: Jesus first; Others second, Yourself last.

It is currently popular in many churches to say, "The church divides the family by having so many meetings. Let's do everything on one night to keep the family together." Numerous congregations and denominations have marriage-enrichment and how-to-parent programs. Further, many churches encourage couples to sing in the choir together, team-teach Sunday school and participate jointly in fellowship groups. Talk to your mate. Talk to your kids. Do things as a family. Whatever you do, put your family first.

And so we feel like selfish spouses and negligent parents if we seek breathing room. Ironically, Southern Baptist counselors Diana and David Garland contend that the current emphasis on family togetherness "may serve not to strengthen families but to raise the stakes even higher."

108

Couples are not only supposed to stay together, but to daily experience intimate sharing, meaningful dialogue and new jokes.

We're not supposed to want to get away from our life partners. Yet cleaving to one's mate does not mean becoming joined at the hip.

### Jim, Alone at Last

The yearning for elbow room runs deep and wide through marriage relationships. Author Lyn Cryderman cites a Louis Harris poll: 63 per cent of working women and 40 per cent of working men said they don't have enough time for themselves. Cryderman's own informal survey of friends and neighbors yielded similar results; the response told him that nearly *"every* married man and woman could use more time alone."

Cryderman tells the story of Jim, who is separated from his wife: "Jim may be a cad for leaving Betty and the kids, but on Sunday morning he can read the paper, take a shower, listen to the stereo and never miss the fight over the free toy in the cereal box... He may miss all the trappings of marriage and family, but a few evenings with a good novel will go a long way toward easing the pain. Or so it seems sometimes from this side of the fence." Lyn, married eighteen years and the father of four, should know.

### A House of One's Own

Significantly, the Harris poll showed the need for solitude to be a greater concern for women than men, particularly women employed outside the home. As Lyn Cryderman points out, his wife, for many years an at-home mother, doesn't have it any better. "If it isn't our youngest banging on the bathroom door begging to use the toilet (which is in use), it's the neighbor's seven-year-old: 'My mom said I could come over here after school 'cause you don't work.' Is it any wonder that after the kids are tucked in and I suggest we walk to the corner cafe for a cup of coffee she says, 'Please, just leave me alone'?''

My daughter has a storybook called *Molly Moves Out*. The story, aside from being charmingly written and illustrated, grabs me every time I read it to Amanda. Molly is the eldest of eight rambunctious rabbit siblings, who plague her by playing with her lipsticks, borrowing her books without asking, squabbling incessantly. Eventually Molly, fed up, announces to her parents that she is leaving. She wants to be alone. With her parents' blessing, Molly moves across the meadow into a house "just big enough for one."

This is the good part. Molly gets to cook everything she likes best. She reads books for hours on end. Her house is just the way she likes it. She even enjoys a housewarming party with her family—who, afterward, go back home.

Sound good?

### The Kite and the Tail

Why is emotional and physical solitude a wistful fantasy for many couples—something we do not actively seek out, but only long for? Partly, we imagine that there'll be plenty of time to be alone once the kids are grown, at which time the house will seem *too* quiet. So we wearily soldier on in our noisy, cramped houses and our noisy, cramped offices, grateful for teeny snatches of solitude—such as taking out the garbage by ourselves.

Yet paradoxically, we may find that if we have *not* taken time for ourselves during the hectic middle years of marriage, we will find ourselves with a marriage as empty as our nest. Breathing room is also growing room.

Anne Mackovic, married twenty-one years, is just beginning a new and satisfying career as a serious artist. She needs the nurture and solidity that a good marriage can provide; yet she and her husband, Bill, are still working out rough spots in their relationship. One of these spots is their differing needs for togetherness and solitude.

"I'm like a kite turned free, and Bill is the tail," Anne says. She is Irish, passionate, creative. Bill is a solid, sometimes stolid engineer who shows his feelings not by the hugs Anne craves, but by keeping her car gassed and oiled.

"We're not around each other *enough*," Anne says. "When we are together, we're in front of the TV. Television is a tremendous robber of time together. Or I'll go into my study and Bill will retreat to the basement. He's down there so much our son calls it 'Dad's condo.' I'd like a little less solitude."

Emotionally, though, Anne is grateful for the space Bill has given her. "He has allowed me to be and do anything I want, and that's a huge gift for someone to give a spouse."

## Distinct, Not Separate

Granting our partners breathing room does *not* mean never seeing them. Episcopal priest Peter Kreitler cautions, "When married couples allow their lives to pass in the night...passage will eventually be booked with a person whose watch is in sync and who will make time for you."

Marriages in which one or both spouses regularly work long hours, travel on business, pursue separate hobbies and communicate by Post-It notes on the refrigerator are in danger of rudderless drifting. We have all known couples of whom we've wondered, When do they *see* each other?

Jeanette and Robert Lauer, in their study of happily married couples, state categorically: "The marriage is less likely to survive when the two spouses pursue many individual activities." While we've seen that every couple needs to choreograph its own dance of solitude and companionship, the important thing, according to the Lauers, "is not that people do particular things apart and together, but that they do something apart and many things together."

Barbara and Jerry Hoffman are a textbook-case match of extrovert and introvert. Barbara has dozens of friends; invariably her telephone line is busy, or she isn't home. Jerry looks a bit like singer John Denver, but it's hard to imagine him doing a Christmas-in-Colorado TV special. It's hard to imagine him watching TV. He'd rather sit upstairs pecking away at his computer.

Barbara puts it this way: "I think of us being in a long, narrow house. I'm on the porch waving and calling 'Hi! Hi!' at people. Jerry's at the end of a long hall, and you have to make an effort to go to him.

"In the early days of our marriage, Jerry was always in his darkroom, and I was always gone. It was a hard moment when, about three years into our marriage, we realized how different we were. He thought, 'Oh no, she's going to drag me to all these things, evening volleyball, vacations with other people.' I thought, 'Not only does he not want to be with other people, he doesn't want to be with me!'

"We've had to work on this, both with each other and with others. And we've had to work on things we can do together. Like church. If we had to go to the coffee hour, adult class and second service, that's

STRONG MARRIAGES, SECRET QUESTIONS

three hours with a lot of people—too much for Jerry, great for me. So we compromised. We go to the early service, where there are fewer people.

Something apart, many things together.

## Breathing the Same Air

My husband and I enjoyed a long courtship. Over the course of our friendship-turned-romance, we spent many, many hours together—taking long exploratory drives in his unpredictable Toyota, seeing every movie that came out, and just sitting for hours over coffee and talking, talking, talking.

Then, we didn't fancy solitude. We'd each had plenty of that as singles. We reveled in our "twoness." If we could have been fused at the hip, we probably would have said, "Sure, if insurance covers it."

Today, twelve years on, I still love to be with my husband, and I miss him when our lives get so hectic we *do* communicate by notes on the kitchen table. But I also need my morning time alone—sometimes, as I've said, I stay in bed; other times I get up first and savor the morning. Fritz needs his time alone cleaning the garage or running out to the store. ("Want me to come along?" "No, that's okay.")

We're better off for these escapes. We tend to be intense, engaged people who love to mix it up emotionally, intellectually, physically. We also have a small house, where "a room of one's own" is a physical impossibility.

Each of us has learned to allow the other those zones of freedom the Lauers speak of. I don't follow him to his weekly basketball games with the guys. He knows better than to come in when I'm performing morning ablutions in the bathroom.

We do share brief prayer at dawn and longer

sitting-together time once prayers are over. Often, he'll sit in the kitchen while I cook dinner. We've learned to ask the other, "Do you want to be by yourself for awhile?"

We know we can always come back together. Not always touching—but together.

---

## Giving Your Spouse More Breathing Room

Couples *can* learn to give each other more physical and emotional solitude. Here are a few suggestions.

◆ Make solitude a priority. Fight for it if you have to. Work it into your daily routine. Each of you needs it. Offer your spouse a gift of time: "Let me take the kids to the park so you can have some time to yourself."

◆ Try to get away—really away—from people. Even if you have your own office or a study at home, you're not really alone when there's clamor right outside your door. Until we're alone and in relative quiet, we have no idea how much we're surrounded by noise and by other people.

◆ Plant a garden. If you have the space, a garden is an ideal place for solitude.

◆ Become involved in separate activities. Don't feel as if you have to double-team on everything.

◆ Talk about your differing needs for solitude and togetherness, but do it gently. Make it clear that your need for time alone isn't a slap at your spouse; you will be a better partner for the refreshment.

◆ Make sure each of you has the necessary balance of

solitude and togetherness. Such things shouldn't be one-sided.

◆ Be aware of signs indicating you need time alone. Irritability, fatigue, forgetfulness—even a stress headache—may be telling you that you need a break. Listen for these signals.

◆ Take time alone to get to know God. Appreciate the beauty of his creation. Learn how to talk to him in prayer, and how to "hear" the answers.

# Chapter Nine
# Are We Still in Love?

*[Older couples] try tell me how this
older, comfortable-slipper love is
much deeper and more fulfilling than
the younger, passionate one; but why
do I always feel as if they're trying to
talk themselves into something they've
heard before but don't really believe?*

John Fischer

A few winters ago my husband and I were in Florida
visiting an old friend of mine. Kate was eight months
pregnant with her second child, but we had a
wonderful time picking up the threads of our
friendship, finding coquina shells on the beach,
dodging flying cockroaches, and looking for the real
Florida of swamps and alligator shows. Kate and
Don had been married eight years at that point, and I
knew their marriage had been rockier than some. But
nothing prepared me for the sound of Kate's weeping
in the night.

My husband and I awoke to hall lights turned on
and a hissing (hers), mumbling (his) argument in the
master bedroom. The next day Kate told us that Don

had confessed to a near-infidelity. He had wandered over to a neighbor's house. The wife was alone. He had been tempted to stay, but instead he came home and said to Kate, "I'm sorry. I screwed up terribly."

The rest of our visit was a time of awkward silences, calculated busyness, cheerful chatter for the sake of the Collinses' toddler son.

The Collinses began marriage counseling. I ached for my old and dear friend, a quite remarkable woman who had put aside a promising academic career to follow her husband to his Florida dream of starting a marina. Kate hated the heat and bugs and overdevelopment. But Kate is strong, perhaps too strong. And I ached for gentle, needy, confused Don. It was not the first time he had been tempted to stray.

More to the point than the near-misses, perhaps, is the tension I sensed in their marriage. Were the Collinses in love at that time? Probably not. What about now?

Kate and I have kept in touch through several moves, more kids, career changes and a shared reaching of forty. The other day we talked on the phone for a very long time. I asked her, "How are things with you and Don?" (Friends of twenty-five years' standing can bring up questions like that.)

"Don and I are really good now," she said. "We've had to work on forgiveness. It's not a magic thing that happens once and for all; it's a process. We can both look back and say, we survived this. We can survive anything." The Collinses can say, Yes, we are still in love—and it means a lot more now.

Married love has to do with going through things together, with, as Daniel O'Leary puts it, discovering new places in the heart created by suffering. And, I would add, by enduring, surviving, growing. Mature married love is something we grow into. It's like the too-large pair of shoes we intentionally buy for our children.

When we marry, the vastness of long-time love doesn't fit us. We aren't ready for it. We love, yes; we take seriously the vows and may even believe that we are receiving a sacrament. But we have to be married a few years—at least ten—before we apprehend the richness and complexity of this love.

It is easier to say what "married in-loveness" is *not*:

◆ It is not romance (though that is a part of it).
◆ It is not commitment (though without it, we don't give love a chance).
◆ It is not sex (which seems to wax and wane according to the season).
◆ It is not companionship (because our spouse is not, and should not be, the only person who fills that role for us).

Nor is it warm feelings. And this is where couples, women particularly, begin questioning. One day we look at our mate and...nothing happens. No rush of feel-good sentiment, no push of desire. Just a shrugging sort of "Well, there he is." Then we worry: What's happened? Has love died?

The fact is that no relationship can long sustain continual heat and fond feelings. Nothing would get done! Passion is by its nature ephemeral, more a physical phenomenon than an act of intellectual volition. Passion is akin to steam bursting out of the ground on Icelandic tundra; passion is like a Perseid meteor flaming across the August midnight. Passion burns itself out and may be mistaken for love. Robert Solomon says, "We too easily tend to conclude that great feeling constitutes love...But this is dangerous nonsense."

### Closed for Lack of Interest?

There's a great line in Terry Pringle's novel *A Fine Time to Leave Me,* the story of a young and troubled marriage: "Lori had become such a common object in her husband's life, she had to beg for his attention." After a couple of years.

Dullness is what people dread most about marriage. Becoming "common objects" to each other, like marital furniture occupying the same house. This is the thing that people try to escape through affairs. We agree that grown-up love means adjusting, making allowances, giving up—and we also wish that, somewhere along the line, marriage could be a whale of a good time.

There was a time I didn't think I wanted to get married. The only younger married people I knew seemed boring and bored. Married men wore plaid pants and played golf; married women drove lumbering station wagons and invited other married women over to see their new avocado kitchens. I could not picture living, forever, with one person; wouldn't life get insufferably tedious? I imagined a life for myself as a single woman writer, living in a thatched English cottage, pouring myself into my art and carrying on a series of bantering, subtly sexy relationships with older men with salt-and-pepper beards. Maybe I'd have a London *pied-à-terre* and conduct lively salons.

Marriage seemed such a constricting way to live, like a narrowed and hardened artery through which blood struggles. I wanted options, choices, the free flow of colors and alternatives through my life.

I still do. I'm not going to say that I gave up all that

childish nonsense, grew up and settled down. I don't have the Devonshire cottage; but I do have my work and my window (and I suppose our house is small enough and old enough to qualify as a cottage). I'm not alone as much as I would prefer; but neither am I lonely. I don't have the salon; but my husband and I do have a large circle of lively friends. Mostly, though, I have the one person who's *there,* who has helped heal old wounds. I've taught him to laugh more and he's taught me to smile more.

Someone has said that marriage keeps mortality at bay, and I think that's true. It may even be literally true: some studies have found that married people suffer from fewer illnesses and have greater longevity than single people.

We have our dull days. We have our dull months. I have my restless wonderings—what would it be like to have had another kind of life? We don't go on date nights or play in the rain very much; we violate all those women's magazine rules on "How to Put Zest Back into Your Marriage."

But we're still married, and there's a sureness about the union: we know this is right. This is *meant.*

Married love at its rare best hides a mystery and paradox at its heart. Tedium and passion intertwine with contentment and questing to create something not quite knowable and very probably holy. Marriage should not always be boring; commitment should not be a prison sentence. Further, two persons should not disappear into marriage—be *Married Beyond Recognition,* as the title of a recent book puts it.

Sooner or later, mature married partners need to come to grips with this wake-up-and-smell-the-coffee reality: There are worse things than being bored. No one ever died of ennui. Our culture has seduced us with the lie that life should be continuously (as in constantly) exciting, varied, stimulating. So husbands and wives flee boredom into sometimes unsavory escapes. It is a great danger when one spouse misinterprets his boredom with himself as boredom with his mate.

Certainly marriage should not be a lifelong boredom. But *periods of dullness,* like periods of grey overcast, are going to happen. Wait. Happiness will come. But Americans don't like to wait. Often, waiting doesn't even occur to us.

Ben Patterson, an author and Presbyterian pastor, tells this story about a counseling session: "I put on my best Carl Rogers counseling demeanor, asked lots of questions, listened sympathetically to all Tom said and fed it back to him. I did everything I could to understand his situation.

"After about an hour and a half of this, I realized Tom wanted to divorce his wife simply because he wasn't happy with her anymore. No cruelty was involved, no adultery—just boredom. I dropped Carl Rogers and tried to talk him out of it, to persuade him to recommit himself, to go the long haul. He listened to me for a while, and then said, 'But Ben, what about happiness?'

"Here's the embarrassing part: I could think of nothing to say to him. It had never occurred to me to tell him that he might have to wait to be happy."

### Eggnogs and Oil Paintings

Louisa Ray has been married seventeen years and is rarely bored. She says *surprise* is important to the vitality of a long-term relationship, and she believes that there can be surprise in a marriage after such a very long time.

"When you first fall in love it's a thrill and a

surprise that here is someone who *likes* you. And then in the middle you take it for granted; you're in a period of struggle and letdown. But then you enter a new phase. This time the surprise comes from the fact that love has grown—that someone knows you so well.

"This is just a small example, but it shows how you can express your love through knowing someone well. Keith likes eggnog, so I buy him eggnog. That's more of a surprise than a birthday gift. You know them better so you can love them in an everyday way; but it's still a surprise that someone has discovered you."

Louisa likens grown-up marriage to an oil painting created with many layers, colors, brushes. Early love, she says, is a quick watercolor.

All this would sound Pollyanna-ish at best (What planet does *she* live on?) and discouraging at worst (Why isn't our relationship like that?) but for one thing: Louisa, like Kate, has known great pain in her marriage. She treasures Keith all the more for almost having lost him.

When they were first married, Keith was heavily involved in a religious group Louisa now calls a "cult"—small, secretive, exclusive, unorthodox by the standards of traditional Christian doctrine. They argued about the cult, and Louisa wondered why she had married this man. "I cried all the time and anguished about what kind of future we'd have."

Keith did leave the cult, which ultimately disbanded. But that wasn't the end of the Rays' problems. Louisa then experienced what she calls a near-miss: a strong attraction to, and growing friendly-but-dangerous involvement with, a man she met while traveling on business. Nothing "happened," but after the trip the man continued to call and write, and it took considerable prayer and toughness for Louisa to resist the allure of a sympathetic and companionable acquaintance—something Keith, at the time, was not.

"Everything was up for grabs," Louisa acknowledges now. "But I think it eventually drew us together. I liken it to being married in wartime, where your safe, secure daily life isn't taken for granted. When you have it, you cherish it."

## In Other Words

*Love* is a big word—maybe too large and diffuse to be helpful as we search for meanings of married in-loveness. More manageable words may help us understand our marriage.

*Cherish* is one. We cherish our heirloom Delft, our old photo albums, our good name. It helps if we see the marriage relationship, its past, present and yet-to-come, as a bright and treasurable thing that can be broken or lost.

*Acceptance* is another. The other night my husband and I were lying in bed, talking deeply and candidly—something we don't do enough these days. I opened my soul to him, speaking of past self-discontents and decisions made to act on those discontents. He listened without comment. Finally he said quietly, "Thank you for telling me those things. I didn't know all that."

Paul Tournier writes that "everyone needs to be understood by at least one other person." My husband understands me; he knows I'm a complicated person. More important, he accepts who I am. Always has. My marriage is one place where I don't feel I'm on some sort of professional or emotional testing ground, proving my worth to the world. Home is where, when you go there, they already *know* you're okay. Sometimes, too often, such familiarity does breed contempt. Acceptance alone degenerates into affectionate boredom. This is the paradox of marriage: much of what is so marvelous about the estate also carries the potential for pain, for the quiet death of love.

Still, had I lived out my original cottage fantasy, the only creature who would have accepted me fully would have been the shaggy terrier I pictured sleeping by the fire of a sleety night. Curly-haired men would have come and gone while I sat at my roll-top desk, thinking great thoughts. All the while growing more eccentric.

Here's another word: *build*. We've noted how the daily grind of "Marriage, Inc.," can wear down a relationship. But I carry in my mind an idealized movie-poster portrait of a strong pioneer couple standing shoulder-to-shoulder, sharing the common task of carving a land out of the wilderness. While the reality of frontier life was grim and often sordid, there is something to the idea of work as the warp and woof of marriage. Kate and Don have renovated houses, stayed up nursing a handicapped child, supported each other through the challenges of new careers and the demands of graduate school. When I'm working with my husband on the household budget, or debating the merits of whole chicken breasts versus cut-up fryers, or deciding what to do about renovating the back porch, it feels like real marriage. It feels like *building* something.

And that takes time. Married love deepens and expands slowly. It reveals its textures subtly. It is no accident that divorce rates drop dramatically after about ten years of marriage. By then couples are growing into their marriages. By then we have *lived* into our marriages.

### Well, What About the Fun?

In Anne Tyler's novel *Breathing Lessons,* Maggie Moran, married forever, remembers how she and her best friend, Serena, made a girlhood promise *never* to put chores ahead of romance in their marriages. Over the years, though, things changed—as they do. As the book opens, Serena is newly widowed, and Maggie is silently asking her, "How long since you saved the dishes till morning so you could be with Max? How long since Max even noticed you didn't?"

This is what most people think of when they ask the are-we-still-in-love question. Most of us probably are like Maggie and Serena. We take care of the mess before we take care of our mates, who most of the time don't care. Often our spouses are right in there cleaning up with us, but rarely do we think about "being with Max." Rarely do we think about simply enjoying our spouses—as we used to do.

I know couples who seem like they were poured from one mold. They laugh together, touch often, look at one another, even refer to the other in conversations with friends. I also know couples who don't seem as if they belong together, but somehow they make it work. And then there are those husbands and wives who seem oddly separated, though married. They rarely talk to or about one another. They shrug and accept the leading of separate lives. Most of their relating is done through chores and children. The man-and-woman spark is missing.

Unfortunately, many long-married couples fall into the third category. Either they've never learned how to be a couple, or they used to know but don't care anymore. Acceptance has atrophied into passive acquiescence. They have forgotten how to cherish their greatest treasure. The shared enterprise has deteriorated into unthinking routine. They're not having much fun.

Every couple will interpret "fun" differently. Kate and Don snuggle in front of the VCR after the kids are in bed. Other couples cook together, subscribe to a theater season or go out to restaurants. "Fun" goes beyond mere shared amusement to a deep enjoyment of the other—whether you're doing dishes together, laughing with your children or simply sitting in companionable silence.

One couple I know are both professors and brilliant scholars, keenly interested in intellectual pursuits. Their friends speculate on the rarefied content of their dinner-table discussions. One day my husband and I happened to find ourselves stuck in traffic behind them on the homeward commute. "Hey, isn't that the Reeds?" he asked. I looked up. "It has to be," I said. "Look at them." The wife was showing her husband a piece of paper—an article or, perhaps, a letter. They were both laughing and smiling at each other. Clearly, they were enjoying each other.

### The Best Is Yet to Be

The fact that we come to this point of asking about the state of our love is probably a good and hopeful sign. The wall is not insurmountable. Still, we must not end with that single question. The response may be facile and reflexive: Of course we're still in love! Case closed. We have to keep probing: Are we still in love? Yes. Is it more than a mere absence of overt hostility? Yes.

Well, then, are we showing it? How? How can we make it better?

And: What is our love like *now*? Have we grown

into our marital pair of shoes? Married love is akin to faith in God, or creative talent, in that the best is dynamic, growing, unfolding. It is not enough to look back at a (probably romanticized) courtship. Love at twenty or twenty-five is not the same, and should not be the same, as love at forty.

At the same time, our early love offers a sort of idyllic template for how good our relationship can be. "Marriage," says author Tim Stafford, "is not God's kingdom, but it teaches us what his kingdom is like." And our memories of courtship can provide a whiff of Eden for our marriage. Recollections of paradise show us what can be. And it helps to remember that we maybe aren't all that old and settled after all.

Because we are committed for a lifetime, we have a great and mysterious hope. Surprises await. The building is not yet topped out; the oil painting is not yet dry. Pain may—will—fill in the secret places of the heart. But if we acknowledge, even celebrate, the paradox of marriage's passion and tedium, solidity and fluidity—and if we affirm, above all, that *this matters more than almost anything else*— nothing will be over. In fact, everything, really, is beginning for us.

---

## Ten Essentials for Keeping Love Alive

Many of us ask the "Are we still in love?" question occasionally. But we are more apt to answer in the affirmative if we follow these basic principles:

◆ *Like* your spouse. Enjoy him or her as a person. No, your spouse doesn't have to be your best friend—but basic compatibility is essential to a strong marriage.

◆ Respect and honor him or her. In the wedding vows we promise to "love, honor and cherish"; too often, however, we forget the second part of the promise. Ask yourself: Do I truly respect my mate as a God-created person of worth and dignity?

◆ Cultivate a rich sexuality. It's too easy to let this area slip, but don't let it happen! The "clean joy" of married sex is a powerful binding force. It also reinforces a privacy and intimacy critical in a good marriage.

◆ Maintain an active and varied life, both together and separately. Work, friends and outside interests enrich the marriage.

◆ At the same time, however, make very sure you have a chunk of time together every day. We underrate our need for simple "hanging around" time together. You don't always have to be conversing or "doing" something. Physical proximity matters.

◆ Hold your tongue. Sticks and stones break your bones, and names *can* harm you—or your spouse. No matter how angry you are with him or her at a given moment, don't say things you may regret later. Despite what some advocates of total openness say, angry words can beget angry feelings.

◆ Learn the virtues of waiting. We all go through dry seasons in our marriages. Generally, though, they don't last. Wait out these seasons—the greening of marital renewal will come.

◆ Love the warts. It is always a shock to discover that your mate is not exactly like you. But *acceptance* means accepting the entire package, quirks and all. You might even try to love those quirks!

◆ Be there for one another. Too many marriages founder

on the issues of trust and dependability. Be emotionally available to your spouse. Do what you say you'll do. Expect the same of him or her.

◆ Regularly thank God for your marriage and your spouse; pray for and with him or her. A good marriage is a priceless gift. Most of us don't appreciate our unions enough. Acknowledge God's hand in your relationship—and share that joy with your spouse.

## Chapter Ten
# Does Faith Really Make a Difference?

*When all these persons and relations
and projects that shape and fill my life
are removed, who or what is left?*

James Fowler

As we get older, we more often are brushed by the wings of our own mortality—through a dream, an illness, an accident or the death of someone our age. Nearly all of us have also paused in a solitary moment and asked: Who or what is left?

Everyone believes in something. We are wired to make sense out of chaos. We may order our world with vague concepts of a force, or love, or nature. We may, like 95 per cent of Americans, believe in "God"—or go further and claim Jesus Christ as the sovereign to whom we declare fealty. However we sort out the universe, by the time we reach our fourth or fifth decade of life we have usually identified what author Marty Martin calls a few "connections, clues, plots."

## What's Good About Getting Old?

I turned forty last year and frankly was surprised at how happy I felt to achieve that venerable estate. I don't want to be twenty again; partly because I weigh less now than I did in college, mostly because I know more. I know what I believe. For me, the connections, clues and plots come together in Jesus Christ, God made man.

I didn't know this at twenty. I knew my sign. I thought I might want to go to Stonehenge and commune with druidic spirits. I had not gone to church in years, not since I was confirmed at age thirteen.

"Christianity" seemed desiccated and dull—a failed, has-been sort of religion. Jesus did not. Once, I had known him. I loved to look at the Warner Sallman print that hung in Sunday school; the idea of Jesus made me feel cozy and cared for.

I wanted that again.

Eventually, I found it. Or he found me. Shortly thereafter, not coincidentally, I met the man who was to become my husband.

I still prize mystery, the hush and tingle of wondering reverence. But I don't worship the *search*. One of my favorite hymns is the early American "How Firm a Foundation." At forty, I'm finally able to make a few here-I-stand affirmations. The solid ground feels real and reassuring.

## An Affirmation

Where I stand today is in the shadow and light of the cross—the shadow, because I'm still amazed, fifteen years after becoming a Christian, that Jesus died for me—and the light, because through Jesus' teachings, sacrificial death and resurrection, I'm pointed toward Truth.

That Truth is this: Because Christ overcame death "with a mighty triumph o'er his foes," in the words of the grand old hymn, we have the promise of more than meaninglessness, more than futile striving and searching. It matters how I live my life, because my life, with him, is going somewhere.

Christianity is about facing up to the darker side in ourselves—the self-centeredness that subtly poisons all our motives (will this make me look good, hey, why not take a picture of me being wonderful?) and limits our horizons to the material world. It's about saying, I don't want that side of myself. I want the sunshine, not the shadow. I want to reach for something better. I won't always achieve it. Often I won't achieve it. But with Christ's help...perhaps I can do a bit better.

So can we all. We cannot do it alone. But when we truly listen to Jesus, when we attend his call to turn from the dark and come to him for a new start, we can become new. Not perfect—but *changed*, and for the better.

Faith can and does strengthen and change marriages. When a couple truly lives out biblical values of mutual respect, lifelong commitment, sacrificial love and sexual fidelity—marriage as God intended it—the union is deepened and blessed.

## The Sun Also Rises

Faith provides the best reason I know for getting up in the morning. The world turns, the sun rises, the phlox in my back garden spread their fragrance. The morning paper *thwaps* on the front porch. The automatic coffeemaker clicks on. The morning star fades before the sun. Here is another day: here, too, is what God has done.

Faith in a created order can and should deepen our

apprehension of the small gifts of simple existence. I have a friend who says she can happily "do nothing" for hours; she sits and looks out her window. She is actually pondering, connecting, loving, in a way.

So it is with a couple I'll call Bob and Sarah Markham. They moved from one of earth's true Edens, British Columbia, to the featureless plain of the upper Midwest a few years ago. They don't complain, though, about the undistinguished topography. Bob talks instead about the school playing field near their house and how they love to stand on it of a fall dusk and watch the air turn purple and the yellow lights of the surrounding houses wink on. Bob and Sarah are *appreciators*. They read widely, attend concerts, enjoy the Sunday funnies, never run out of things to talk about.

Bob and Sarah are mature, vibrant Christians. While they have some prickly areas in their fifteen-year marriage (who doesn't?), their faith—and natural imagination and curiosity—has made them salute the small things: a Midwestern baseball diamond, the antics of "Calvin and Hobbes."

One of my favorite lines of Scripture is "God saw that it was good." When a husband and wife also see that goodness, when they share awe and amusement and a good cup of coffee—their union will come a bit closer to what God intended. They'll have more to talk about. And, through these things which are not God but which point to him, they will be brought closer to the Creator.

## The Stalking Pestilence of Discouragement

Sometimes it is difficult to find joy in the paper thumping on the front porch. Discouragement wears us down. We lose heart. I had a spell like that a few months ago. I had sprained my ankle.

Professional projects were languishing. My four-year-old was acting more like fourteen. I got the flu. Then I got stung by a yellow jacket for the first time in my life. By then I was so depressed that the sting seemed like a personal affront—like a little buzz of the demonic.

Someone has said the devil's most powerful weapon is discouragement—which may lead to quick and destructive palliatives. During our times of weariness and doubt, my husband and I have recognized this and have sought God's sustaining protection. And we have talked about evil and the chinks through which it wafts into a soul.

Couples *must* recognize and confront the bad things. However we name the "pestilence that stalks at noonday" or the cold, cold wind that comes in through the cracks, we've all known it.

For Craig and Andrea Vandenberg, the dark thing actually wears the face of pestilence. Andrea suffers from systemic lupus erythematosus, a mysterious and incurable chronic disease of the immune system. Lupus, which causes symptoms ranging from fatigue to joint pain to kidney ailments to psychosis, strikes mainly women of childbearing age; Andrea was a young mother of three when she contracted the illness. For Andrea, lupus means daily naps, fear of sunshine, periodic trips to the Mayo Clinic and anxiety about a crippled old age.

The Vandenbergs have been married eighteen years. They have fared better than some couples stalked by lupus (*lupus* is Latin for "wolf"); Craig told me that about 70 per cent divorce. The Vandenbergs are different; they glow with an inner health, a playful contentment. Craig explains: "A whole theme of these past six years has been unraveling what grace is all about. It's a strange sensation, a crisis like this. Everyone's focused on you, sorry for you—and in a spiritual way you realize that other people can embody Christ to you."

Craig and Andie know that, barring an unforeseen cure, the lupus is not going to go away. They avoid platitudes like "God used the lupus to strengthen our marriage." Indeed, says Craig, "God hates lupus." He wonders whether they will see their fortieth anniversary. Andie worries about losing her hair and gaining weight, side effects of medication. But for the Vandenbergs, life has taken on a certain "brilliance." "We now see things in four-color, not two-color," says Craig. The Vandenbergs continue to hail the sunrise.

### Where Is God When the Faucet Drips?

For some, the stalking thing wears the face of disease; for others, it's alcoholism or abuse or job loss. These are the marital equivalents of Job's boils. This is the problem of pain that theologians have wrestled with down through the centuries. Less clear, however, is the connection between faith and quotidian annoyance—call it "the problem of bills" or (with apologies to Philip Yancey) "where is God when the faucet drips?" How does God undergird a marriage beset by irritants?

According to Lindy and Marshall Garrison, God *is* there when the faucet drips or the drain clogs. Marsh and Lin have been married sixteen years. Marsh is a newspaperman, rumpled yet keenly observant; Lin is a pretty, fresh-faced preschool teacher. The Garrisons have two young boys. They recently moved into a bigger house, and they feel chronically strapped for money and time. They struggle with envy, what Marsh calls the "how-do-they-do-it?" question. Both work, sometimes long hours, in altruistic but low-paying professions. One son has allergies. Not dire difficulties, but the kind of continual annoyance that can erode a marriage.

Their marriage has not eroded. More than many other couples whose marriages have passed the decade mark, the Garrisons are openly romantic and clearly enjoy one another. Why? "We start at the same point: our faith," says Marsh. "Our faith, our commitment to each other, and a certain unselfishness. I don't want things for me, I want them for Lin and Ryan and Josh. Lin's the same way. She longed for a bigger house—for all of us." Marsh is emphatic on the need for married partners to put each other first.

The Garrisons have taken their faith beyond a two-dimensional "Jesus and me" mentality and moved to a generous inclusiveness that seeks to serve the other. The way the Garrisons—and other couples whose relationships rest on the rock of faith—weather the dripping of daily life is by first asking, "How are *you* doing?"

What this says is: We're in this together. I may want to sleep in on a wintry Saturday, but my husband has to play basketball at 7:30, so I get up with him. He may want to go downstairs to rearrange the basement, but he'll set aside his work to critique a chapter of a work-in-progress.

Selfishness is the greatest enemy of a marriage. Faith makes it easier to ask the other how he's doing and what you can do for him.

## Handing It Over

Faith makes it easier, not easy. This is where prayer comes in—the chance to hand something, like one's struggles with selfishness, over to God. The Garrisons pray every day. Once Marsh had to fire

STRONG MARRIAGES, SECRET QUESTIONS

someone at work. It was one of the hardest things he has ever done, but he knew Lin was praying for him, and it helped.

My husband and I try to maintain an early-morning ritual of prayer. Coffee mugs at hand, we commit the day and each other to the Lord. Usually we pray through a list of concerns, needs, confessions and praises—always praises. It's hard at times not to feel perfunctory about this, as if we're quickly discharging a morning duty: brush teeth, shave, pray. But "duty" isn't always a dirty word. Our prayer time gives us a refreshing pause in the morning rush; yet it has little to do, really, with what's good for us. It has everything to do with an old-fashioned word we don't hear much any more: obedience. I don't necessarily "feel" any better after I pray. That's not the point. The point is that God asks his people to pray, and he has promised to listen.

### Why Church Matters
Of course, no marriage thrives in isolation. No matter how satisfying our union, we need other people in our lives—healthy relationships with friends who affirm most of the same values we do. The best place to find those people is in church.

When I was growing up in the fifties, attending church was What You Did. People didn't talk about "being a Christian," they talked about "going to church." That's changed. While a sizable majority of Americans claim membership in a religious body, less than half actually go regularly. Church attendance and involvement have become optional.

They shouldn't be. Counselor Paul Mickey is insistent on the need for husband and wife to worship together. "In this way," he says, "they will be in a position to develop spiritually at a comparable pace, they'll be working arm-in-arm toward the same spiritual goals at the institution of their choice; and they'll relate jointly to a broader spiritual support community."

When a church is doing its job, no institution offers a stronger network of support and caring. In both the dark times and the sunlit times, the friendship of fellow Christians is an incalculable gift to a marriage. John Timmerman, a professor whose wife, Pat, was hospitalized for depression, says this: "At a time when one finds it difficult to pray, because of anxieties, pressure or uncertainties, that person needs a body of committed believers lifting up those anxieties, pressures and uncertainties to the Lord."

I have seen the church we attend hold a prayer vigil for a critically ill child. I have seen recovering alcoholics find meaning and dignity—and in return offer it to other strugglers. I have watched a troubled newcomer to a prayer group weep and be comforted.

I have also seen simple offers of help and encouragement for everyday problems. Friends have said to me, "You're working so hard; let us baby-sit so you two can get out." Men barter services: wallpapering for rewiring.

It's also fun to give back some of what church gives you. My husband and I have led toddler and preschool groups; for us, doling out bug juice and Teddy Grahams and playing Duck-Duck-Goose were as good as a date night. On the way home we looked at each other and said, "You know, that was fun. We should do more of that!" I know couples who work at shelters for battered women, take in troubled teenagers, help people move. Others are intensely involved in small groups.

How involved to get in a church is a point of contention for many couples. Hal, an executive for a Christian organization, and his wife, Sue, recently joined a lively, youthful church aimed at the young professionals of their suburban area. Sue has plunged into church life. Hal, however, resists, citing natural introversion and a belief that his ministry with his organization is his way of serving God. They have not yet resolved their differences.

Nora and Stan Paczynski would envy their problems. They are shopping for a church; Stan was not comfortable in their former congregation and Nora wants to share church involvement with her husband. "It's scary how easy it is *not* to go to church," she said to me the other day. "Last Sunday I slept late. We didn't know where to go, so I said to Stan, 'Oh, let's just not go.' He was happy to have a free Sunday."

## The Soul of the Matter

Poet, preacher and storyteller Walter Wangerin, Jr., tells the story of a deep rift that occurred between him and his wife, Thanne, some years ago. He was a pastor then, rushing to fulfill his duties to "his" people, spinning magnificent sermons, reading books on deep spiritual subjects. Thanne was home with four small children, one of them hyperactive.

Wrapped up in his calling, driven to perform, Walt was insensitive to his wife's emotional needs, and, in his blindness, he did her grave harm—teasing her in front of friends, embarrassing her from the pulpit. Finally Thanne, not an overly emotional person, could take it no longer. Hurt beyond words, she would for weeks exchange only the minimum of civilities with her husband. The marriage seemed riven beyond healing. Since divorce was not an option, Wangerin resigned himself to a lifetime of lovelessness.

And then something happened.

One day Thanne came quietly into her husband's study. "Wally," she began, "will you hug me?"

She forgave.

Or, more accurately, says Wangerin: "Thanne could not forgive me. But Jesus could."

Often, often in marriage are we called to forgive—and to be forgiven, which in some ways is harder. We do awful things to each other, and we feel unworthy; in Wangerin's words, we feel like "walking faults." We want to do better. Next time we will not say the wounding word, make the costly checkbook error, disappoint our child.

But we may not do better next time. We may learn to keep accurate financial records, but some other weed will spring up in our marital patch. This is where the forgiveness of Christ takes over and enables us to say to our spouse, "You don't *have* to do better, to 'improve.' I accept and love you for who you are, weeds and all." Because we have Christ's assurance of forgiveness, because we feel his unconditional love, we can, in turn, love and forgive.

And another thing. When we are helped to forgive through the grace of God, when we reconcile with our mates despite the huge, horrible things and the tiny, nasty things (and I have seen some remarkable reconciliations following some very great wrongs), we are recommitting ourselves to our spouses. We may stand up in public and make our sacred vows once. But every day—*every day*—a rich, strong, imaginative faith can help us to act those vows again.

## How the Two of You Can Cultivate a Spiritual Life

◆ Read the Bible. Find out what God has to say about men and women in marriage, about human nature, and about how God wants people to live.

◆ Pray for each other, and with each other. There are no special techniques which you need to learn to make prayer "work." God is listening and acting. In different ways he will provide answers.

◆ If you enjoy singing, occasionally sing hymns together—in the car, while doing chores, and so on. Singing is a joyful way to exalt God, and it is uplifting to celebrate his care and concern for us.

◆ Share your faith with your children by your lifestyle as well as in direct teaching. Make sure that both of you are taking the lead in this. As you teach your children, so you will learn.

◆ Get into the habit of regularly thanking God for the many good things in your lives; confess your failings and ask forgiveness; share your problems and seek his help.

Chapter Eleven

# Will My Dreams Ever Come True?

*The biggest human temptation is...to settle for too little.*

Thomas Merton

Emily Dickinson called hope the "thing with feathers." This fluttering marvel enables Cub fans to greet every April with joy. Hope heartened my husband years ago as he watched his father's protracted dying from cancer: "We kept hoping they'd find a cure," he said.

Even the word is pretty: *hope*.

Hope drives dreams. And who, with the possible exception of a mother gazing at her newborn, holds the thing with feathers more tenderly than a couple joining their dreams at the altar?

## Why Do We Always Think Small?
Then the career derails, the children don't come (or come and are less perfect than we fancied), health abandons us. Or our spouse, obscurely, disappoints us—sometimes without even knowing it. In fact, our

spouse surely *will* disappoint us. He'll behave embarrassingly; she'll gain weight; he'll cut corners in business; she'll lose interest in sex.

A friend of mine says that disappointment in our spouse almost always masks disappointment in ourselves. Possibly. But here is the most universal cry: Where did all the dreams go? It's less a shattering than a slow greying of the vividness. Once we dreamed of writing books that would touch millions; now we are writing technical manuals. Once we spun fancies of rosy, happy children; now the school counselor is telling us our adopted son is hyperactive. In other words, our lives are not what we had hoped years ago when we and life were green with promise. We cope. But we wonder: Can't *one* thing come out the way it was supposed to? Why do we always have to think small?

Last Christmas my husband and I heard from a friend, Wes, whom we'd lost touch with over the years. His letter was mostly joy and faith—a flourishing twenty-year marriage, three strapping sons—but Fritz and I both detected a shadow of wistfulness. He had dreamed of beginning his own small but select publishing house. He had dreamed of making an impact. That had not, as yet, happened. At forty-five Wes remained a middle-level editor. Life was good, but this man, talented and full of ideas, was softly disappointed. And we, caring about this friend, were grieved. Between the lines of his letter, this: *I wonder if it will ever happen?*

I also watched *It's a Wonderful Life* last Christmas. I always do. But this time I noticed something different about the film. It is generally thought of as a warm-hearted celebration of the difference just one person can make. It is that; yet there's also a bittersweet edge to the story. George Bailey desperately wanted to escape stifling Bedford Falls and "lasso the moon." Instead, he got stuck, averting financial ruin only through divine intervention. George Bailey was not a failure, but I often wonder if he ever made it to Paris—or if the call of a distant train whistle ever made him think about his teenage hopes.

## Everything But Boils
Then there are the absolute disappointments, the crashing tragedies that in an individual life are the equivalent of George Orwell's boot of tyranny stomping on a human face—forever. They cannot be explained away. They kill the thing with feathers.

Yet the maimed have much to teach us.

I've never known anyone who has suffered quite as much as Amy Harris. Amy grew up in a dysfunctional family. Her father was an alcoholic. Her first marriage ended in divorce. She discovered she was unable to bear children. Then she met Garry, a writer twenty years her senior. He was also divorced, with grown children. His books had not sold well; to make things worse, he had been financially irresponsible and had incurred huge debts.

But Amy and Garry fell in love and were married. Amy, a small-business owner, worked hard to pay off Garry's debts. He wrote a book that sold fairly well and they bought a house on Michigan's Upper Peninsula. "People finally started to believe we were going to make it," she says.

They had just celebrated their third anniversary when Garry suffered a stroke, which left him partially paralyzed. Worse, it affected the areas of his brain governing emotion and creativity. Several years of intensive (and costly) therapy have not helped. He is unable to write; he cannot love Amy. She in turn cares about him in a fond, parental way. In her mind, the marriage is over. Garry now resides in a permanent-care facility near Chicago, where a sister lives.

Meanwhile Amy, who owes various creditors including the Internal Revenue Service many thousands of dollars, has declared bankruptcy (which still doesn't protect her from the IRS, to whom bankruptcy is no excuse not to pay). She was unable to sell the house in the depressed economy of the U.P. Instead, she lost it when the bank foreclosed on the mortgage. She doesn't even have a business to run anymore: she liquidated everything in an effort to pay off her debts. Though weight has always been a problem for her, she now fights a tendency to be anorexic.

Today Amy is doing free-lance consulting, living in a small apartment and trying to rebuild her life. Slowly.

"Amy—you're like Job, except without the boils," I said to her recently.

She laughed. "The way my face is breaking out, I may have those too!"

Most of us, thankfully, will not endure half of what Amy has suffered. Yet she can still let rip with *bons mots*. Deeply Christian, she has not wavered in her faith. Her voice wavers a lot—of course. She weeps often—of course. But she prays more than she weeps. Of course.

While Amy's plight is far more grievous than that of Wes, the disappointed editor, her insights apply to anyone who feels life has dealt them an unfair hand— or, to put it in terms of faith, who wonders in what cave God has concealed himself. This is what she said:

"If you are a person of faith, as I am, you have to know where you are going. We are 'strangers and pilgrims' in this world, the Bible says. No: When we suffer major tragedy or disappointment, our emotions will not 'get better' for a long time. But it may help to remember our ultimate destination.

"Practically, we have to get up and *fight!* Go beyond commiserating. The Lord has given us things to do. You can hurt, but you can keep on working, even through the hurt.

"Also, we forget something: We're not on earth to have a happy marriage. When I see people in happy marriages, I pray, 'Lord, let them realize this incredible gift they have.' Marriage is the starting point out of which we serve. It should not be our focus.

"And in everything we need to realize the underlying importance of redemption. We go through lots of little resurrections in our lives and in our marriages. 'Just As I Am' should be the theme at every wedding. God allows awful things to happen so we can experience these little rebirths. Some flowers perish with too much sun.

"We're so afraid of pain. I'm in so much pain that sometimes it hurts to breathe. But as I said, you have to live *through* the hurt."

## Admiring the Struggle

The fact is, if Amy can survive everything but boils, those of us whose disappointments are George Bailey-sized can too. And we can help our partners through the death of *their* dreams. We can help them hear the song of the thing with feathers.

Indeed, this is one of the most compelling tasks of marriage: to help the other hope, to hearten the weary, to build up the shriveled in spirit.

Author Cynthia Spence writes eloquently of her husband's career problems. While she had pursued an editorial career and met mostly straight-line success, his had been a working life of detours and potholes and wrong turns. They argued—a lot. Things came to a head one night when Craig lashed out, "You don't know what it's like for me because you've never failed!"

"Craig had opened the door to his heart, and I had fallen in," Cynthia Spence writes. "I found it a very lonely, frightening, discouraging place to be." Unable to sleep that night, she rose at five, walked and prayed and walked some more. Several blocks from her house she came to this realization: she could respect Craig *for his struggle.* Few others were reaching out to him; some people were not-so-subtly critical of what they perceived as his vocational failures. Craig had been waging a lonely, valiant battle; it was his wife's task to bring in emotional reinforcements.

Another husband, a man who resigned his teaching post after a painful conflict with the school administration and has begun a new career, knows how Craig feels. "Society places such a premium on 'success,'" he says. "And when you lose a job, you're viewed as the opposite of successful—whatever that is. But if you look around, you see a lot of people who are only marginally successful. So why feel that bad?

"You know," he mused, "the spouse who supports her mate may think she's just being 'faithful over a little,' in Jesus' words. But in reality she is doing something very important."

This is not to say that we meekly support our spouses if they are pursuing harebrained schemes. We can try to offer constructive, patient, well-timed advice. Most important, through it all, budding dream or withering disappointment, we can affirm *them*. The husband who quit teaching says, "We desperately need perspective on what's failure and what's not. A psychologist has said that part of the problem today is that we compare ourselves to impossible models. If we have business ambitions, we want to be as successful as Malcolm Forbes was. If our goal is to be an actor, we want to be a star the magnitude of Elizabeth Taylor. We even think maybe we could be President someday."

This wise man, married to an equally astute and devoted wife, may be disappointed over a career that did not turn out the way he hoped. But his is a sort of George Bailey story come to life: his wife, children, many caring friends, and the opportunity to exercise his talents in new ways have made him realize that "it's a wonderful life" after all.

## The Yellow Brick Road

"Dreams we did not discuss, they were embarrassing in normal conversation, especially big ones," writes Garrison Keillor of his determinedly average Minnesota boyhood. The mindset, he says, was: Who do you think you are? Quit loafing around reading a book and go do something useful.

Keillor, of course, knew better. He—unlike George Bailey—did not get stuck in Bedford Falls or Lake Wobegon. He went to the Twin Cities, turned arty and eventually became a famous radio personality. Keillor, then and probably now, was not embarrassed by dreams. Nor should we be.

With one caution, says Colorado psychiatrist and marriage counselor Louis McBurney. Unhealthy *expectations*—dreams' shirttail relatives—can set us up for disappointment. "I see this all the time in my counseling," he says. "People even expect a different kind of *person* than the one they get—maybe they expect their spouse will be like Mom or Dad. Courtship is the great deception, where we're all doing our best to convince the other person that we're wonderful. You have to realize, going into marriage, that these traps are going to be there, and not let yourself get waylaid."

Some people, McBurney adds, seem to "go from one unrealistic fantasy to the next. But I've also known people to dream and *use* their fantasies. Dreams can be a way to get over early-life disappointments and rejections."

McBurney himself admits to being a bit of a dreamer. He recently finished an imaginative novel, now under consideration by a publisher. He and his wife, Melissa, who counsels with him, continue to nurture dreams of practicing medicine among the Third World poor. Even so, Melissa notes, it's important in a marriage to strip off all expectations, dreams and disappointments and get down to the one thing that really matters—what the ancient Greeks called "knowing the one big thing." She says, "I know one thing for sure: I'm supposed to be married to Louis. That's all." When we view dreams—or their death—in that light, it may help ease disappointments.

## Rust Never Sleeps

Disappointment is insidious. It can corrode a marriage like rust eats away at a car, until one day the rear bumper falls off. Many couples, tragically, are *not* brought closer together by suffering. A spouse's unemployment, chronic illness, the loss of a child—these things kill marriages. The divorce rates following the death of a child, or the onset of cancer, are astonishing and disheartening.

149

For other couples, it's the disappointments of too little money, too many kids, not enough fun. "You hear that it's the little things like leaving the cap off the toothpaste tube that affect marriages," said a friend of mine. "I don't think so—at least not for my husband and me. It's the big stuff that gets to us."

The more subtle disappointments—"this person is not what I had hoped for and *I* am not what I hoped for"—can be equally devastating. Disappointment particularly lurks around the corners of middle life. Not all of us have mid-life crises—some of us today have babies instead. But by forty or forty-five, most of us can point to regrets, opportunities missed, parts of our story that have not come out exactly right.

This is where, as Amy notes, a spiritual perspective keeps things in balance. Yet we who are Christian have our own set of problems to deal with. How often we hear a litany like this: "I did everything right. I prayed, read the Bible, went to church, tried to be a good person, partner and parent—and this *still* happened." Louis McBurney says that some people "set themselves up for tremendous disappointment" by these expectations. Faith does not *prevent* disappointment. Properly understood, however, faith should help us when the sadness comes—whether that sadness is in ourselves or things external.

Faith does not deny disappointment. Some things really are awful. I have often felt that the ancient Irish practice of "keening"— sustained high wailing—after the death of a loved one is much healthier than hushed, pious rationalizations that try to make everything have a positive reason— "God is using this to make you stronger" or some such. Weeping and gnashing of teeth may at times be the most satisfying response to a disappointment.

Provided that our spouse is keening along with us; and provided that, once mourning is past, we do get up and fight.

We may place our hope in many things: ourselves, our spouse, our children, our careers, our health. All these are fine. It is good to have many sources from which hope springs. Yet these things also have their limitations. Spouses and children, being human, will disappoint. Careers change. Health fades.

But God doesn't.

Ultimately, then, our hope is in him. It's important to remember that he is in us when we hurt. It is, perhaps, even more important to remember that he is also in our spouse. Amy is right: she has learned, through almost unbearable pain, that a good marriage is an incredible gift. To that I would add: an okay marriage has an incredible potential.

Good marriages can be shaken to their foundations by disappointment. But the couples I've observed who have come through to the other side (or are coping in the midst of struggle) have done so first by God's grace, and second by holding firmly to each other. They have affirmed that the "we" is stronger than the "it" of disappointment. And they have held fast to dreams, driven by that fluttering feathered thing.

Hope.

---

### Nurturing Your Dreams, Healing Your Disappointments

How can you nurture dreams? How can you deal with disappointment? Here are a few suggestions.

151

◆ When you feel disappointed in your mate or your marriage, look closely at *yourself*. "One of the things that helps me put disappointment in perspective is to look at my own faults and shortcomings," says Louis McBurney. "Then I can see Melissa's side better." If you're feeling let down by your spouse, remember that he or she may be feeling equally let down by you.

◆ Be open about your disappointments. Try to say to your partner, "It really disappointed me when you did that"—and say it right away. Careful, sensitive probing—and especially *listening*—may help. Your spouse may have no idea what you're feeling. Small disappointments may fester and turn into big problems. Use a bit of preventive medicine.

◆ Acknowledge that sometimes life stinks, and go on from there. Focus not on what *can't* be, but what can be. I can never have straight hair, short of annihilating it with chemicals. My husband can never be Donald Trump (thank goodness). We can achieve other dreams together.

◆ Do, of course, have individual and mutual dreams that you hold tenderly. It's helpful to discuss occasionally where you want to be in ten or twenty years. Do this in a playful, imaginative way; retirement planning is for another conversation.

◆ Be each other's cheerleaders. Encourage, sometimes challenge each other; speak proudly (never disparagingly) of your mate to others. When we deeply feel our spouse's support, disappointment cuts less.

◆ Remember that sometimes it is enough simply to hold your spouse when he or she is feeling sad or without hope. No one else can do that as well.

Chapter Twelve

# Is It Worth It?

*September, early.*

Now it is the season of butterflies on the wind. For some mysterious reason, this has been a very good year for butterflies: brave monarchs and dauntless red admirals and tiger swallowtails as big and bright as canaries. And now, at this strange, not-quite-summer, not-quite-autumn pause in the year, the butterflies drift by. Cued by an ancient and unfathomable clock, they sense the north wind starting to stir and they flee before it, riding the air currents miles, miles to places where winter is a rumor. They will not return.

I am always moved by the spectacle of a tiny, nearly weightless thing, no more than a bright scrap, really, fluttering over some impossible place—an eight-lane expressway, for instance—and making it. They have *everything* going against them—cars going too fast, hostile weather, hungry birds, their own fragility. Yet they keep flying.

So weak, so tough; so threatened, so astonishing.

Like marriage.

Reason tells us that butterflies shouldn't make it from Chicago to Cancun. But they do. Common sense tells us that one man and one woman shouldn't live a lifetime in complicated, resilient joy—after all, according to some anthropologists, lifelong monogamy is unnatural to the species. We're not Canada geese or African lions. But countless men and women do reach the end of this journey and declare that, yes, marriage was good.

So astonishing.

So threatened. In sorrow I predict that America in the year 2020 will be a place of too many single seventy-year-olds dwelling in burglar-proof, climate-controlled apartments, drawing a subsistence living out of a bankrupt Social Security fund. Most will not be widowed. The bright, soaring expectations they once had, as members of a generation that refused to age gracefully, will be as faded as the old Rolling Stones album covers moldering in a closet somewhere.

If current trends hold up, fewer people will marry; fewer people will stay married. The median duration of an American marriage (for couples marrying today) is a scant seven years. And as the sins of the parents are visited on the children, the picture grows gloomier still; the children of today's divorcing couples are significantly more likely to split up.

But what of our marriages?

In marriage, longevity tends to be rewarded in that the risk of divorce drastically decreases after ten or fifteen years. But we are impatient. We don't want to hang around fifteen years in what seems to us an intolerable—or boring—situation. It doesn't take long for us to start asking the "Is that all there is?" question. And sometimes we don't like the answer.

In this book I have tried to sort out the questions that have an answer from the ones that don't. Some questions hang in the air, like a ringing in the ears that never quite goes away. *Will we ever have enough time?* Yes, but not for many years. *What if I fall in love with someone else?* You may. Live with the pain and paradox and know that feelings are often illusory. *Will my dreams come true?* Possibly not. *Does faith really make a difference?* Yes—but not necessarily in ways we expect.

Here is the great and healing comfort: None of us is alone in asking these questions. I was frankly startled by the depth of struggle and uncertainty in some of the women and men I talked with. I had not expected to hear some of the cries that rose unbidden out of polite conversation. But I was also awed by the heroic, often lonely battles many people are waging against the insidious serpent voices that whisper, *You don't have to live with this, you know. Life's too short; pain can be banished.* Or another whisper, the smug and shattering *What's wrong with you? Why can't you solve this? Everyone else has.*

I began this book with the hunch that marriage is far more complex, at once harder and easier, than we imagine. I conclude this book confirmed over and over again in my hunch. My own experience has done that. The couples who opened up corners of their lives to me did that.

But I also end this book angry. When we tell couples, "Everything will be fine as long as you don't let the sun go down on your anger" or "I *used* to have that problem, but now..." or "Always remember to put your family first," we do untold harm in the name of well-meaning advice.

More subtly harmful than the advice itself are the images of near-perfection such advice conjures up. We think that somewhere there lives a couple who are doing everything right. They might squabble occasionally, but they always fight fair, never send "you-messages" and never go to bed mad. The husband enjoys a group of supportive male friends with whom he has regular breakfasts; these men talk openly about their marriages and hold each other accountable. The wife works part-time but is always home when the kids return from school, because the children can't wait to talk about their day. The couple enjoys weekly nights out and quarterly weekend getaways, at which time they discuss their marriage and set goals for the coming year. They have pulled the plug on television and enjoy lively family dinners, complete with conversation starters. A large and varied group of friends is constantly dropping in. The baby sitter is always available. The grass is always cut. They bought a Victorian house at just the right time, before prices went through the roof, and restored it to perfection. "We used to struggle with home repairs," they say, "but now we always know exactly what to do, and renovating a house strengthened our marriage." The money they save by doing their own repairs goes into a special fund to help underprivileged children.

Do you know anyone like this? Neither do I. Yet their specter hovers around every marriage.

We need to allow ourselves to be real. I have come to realize what a generous gift honesty is. We need to talk with each other. Many couples feel terribly alone. We need to tear down our self-satisfied facades and reveal the rubble that is sometimes in our hearts. We need to provide that intent, engaged, compassionate friendship and support to other men and women.

It's not easy to do.

As a writer, I'm gifted at listening, observing, asking leading questions. I'm less skilled at jumping into the fray. I want the world to think my marriage is stable (which it is), satisfying (which it usually is), exciting (which it sometimes is not). I want to preserve our privacy. And yet I also know that in the name of pride and privacy, isolated marriages have slowly withered until there was nothing left. And everyone says, "We didn't know."

*How* do we accomplish this Sisyphean task of getting couples to open up with each other? First, one at a time—friend to friend. Then couple to couple. Then, perhaps, in a small group or marriage-enrichment setting. And, often, such candor has to come about as the byproduct of a close relationship, not the reason for it.

Or such vulnerability can sneak in through the back door—through humor. Men in particular can be threatened by too much self-revelation, but all of us cringe a bit when it comes to talking candidly about our marriages, our money, our dreams and disappointments.

Beyond talk, there's doing. Again—in our churches, our neighborhoods (for those of us who actually know our neighbors), friends at work, wherever—I would advocate more swapping of favors. I baby-sit for your children; you help with my taxes. I help you move; you tell me where I can find a good used personal computer.

In times not so long past, such bartering was integral to the fabric of the community. I can remember my parents casually saying to apartment neighbors, "Can you run over and watch the kids for a few moments?" Today, our tendency is to buy this kind of help. But tangible, hands-on expressions of support are another way to make a couple feel a bit less alone. They also give a husband and wife an excuse for doing something for someone else—

which can cement a marriage more than almost anything else.

So: be real, be open, do for others, let others do for you and, throughout it all, laugh. A lot.

The healthiest couples I interviewed were those who punctuated their remarks with wisecracks, understood each other's humor and frequently dissolved into laughter. Because life is funny. I don't laugh at television comedians or jokes people tell. I laugh at my husband's awful boat shoes that are splitting their seams. He laughs at my description of some funny incident at work. We both laugh with our daughter when she pretends to be a rock star (and are overjoyed that she seems to be developing the same sort of humor).

Laughter, as we now know, is a powerful healer. It is also a powerful, and underrated, bonding agent. There's a feeling of closeness that's almost sexual when we share a private joke with another person— we've all had the experience of sitting in a roomful of people when something happened that struck us and only one other person there as amusing. Instant rapport. We should strike the same spark with our spouses.

Marriage is precious, important, God-given, worth saving. The reasons for the declining number of marriages today are too complex to go into here. Perhaps couples need to start from the first principle that "this is worth it." Most—not necessarily all—of the husbands and wives I talked to did begin with that assumption. Most of them would say that marriage is God-given and God-ordained. It is not just a social nicety. When a man and a woman have committed themselves to each other, marriage becomes the way in which they develop their potential to live as God intended, to find both purpose and fulfilment. And we cannot afford only to treasure marriage when it is shiny and new. Over the years, the treasure has to be dusted, polished, cradled in our hands and admired regularly. If the treasure shatters, we need to find the epoxy that will glue it back together—and not be ashamed of the cracks.

Alas, I've seen damaged butterflies. Once a tiger swallowtail died in our driveway, probably stunned by a car. I had my husband gently bury it in our garden. Butterflies cannot be put back together again. But the butterfly of a marriage *can* be. And I'm not just talking about facing the dramatic crises that we all read about. I'm talking about always, every day, through the grind and the irritations. I'm talking about little forgivenesses, little re-commitments, medium-sized reconciliations, large acceptances.

Most of the couples I talked with are, I think, doing just that. I salute them; I pray for them; I learn from them. They're a valiant bunch.

Marriage is hard and getting harder. Yet it's possibly the highest expression of raw faith in creation—in things going forward, in God's continuing love—that a man and woman can make. It's worth all the questions we ask.

# Bibliography

Ray Bradbury, *Dandelion Wine* (New York: Bantam, 1967).

Annie Dillard, *Pilgrim at Tinker Creek* (New York: Harper & Row, 1974).

James M. Fowler, *Stages of Faith* (San Francisco, Calif.: Harper & Row, 1981).

George Gallup, Jr., and Jim Castelli, *The People's Religion* (New York: Macmillan, 1989).

Diana S. Richmond Garland and David E. Garland, *Beyond Companionship* (Philadelphia, Pa.: Westminster, 1986).

Andrew M. Greeley, *Confessions of a Parish Priest* (New York: Pocket Books, 1987).

Howard and Jeanne Hendricks and LaVonne Neff, eds., *Husbands and Wives* (Wheaton, Ill.: Victor Books, 1988).

Garrison Keillor, *We Are Still Married* (New York: Viking, 1989).

Peter Kreitler and Bill Bruns, *Affair Prevention* (New York: Macmillan, 1981).

Jeanette C. Lauer and Robert H. Lauer, *'Til Death Do Us Part* (New York: Harrington Park Press, 1986).

Gordon Macdonald, *Rebuilding Your Broken World* (Nashville, Tenn.: Thomas Nelson, 1988)

Martin E. Marty, *A Cry of Absence* (San Francisco, Calif: Harper & Row, 1983).

Paul A. Mickey and William Proctor, *Tough Marriage* (New York: William Morrow, 1986).

Harold Myra, *Love Notes to Jeanette* (Wheaton, Ill.: Victor Books, 1979).

M. Scott Peck, *The Road Less Traveled* (New York: Simon & Shuster, 1978).

Maxine Rock, *The Marriage Map* (New York: Dell, 1986).

Robert Solomon, *About Love* (New York: Simon & Shuster, 1988).

John Taylor, *Circus of Ambition* (New York: Warner Books, 1989).

John H. Timmerman, *A Season of Suffering* (Portland, Ore.: Multnomah, 1987).

Anne Tyler, *Breathing Lessons* (New York: Alfred A. Knopf, 1988).

Walter Wangerin, Jr., *As for Me and My House* (Nashville, Tenn.: Thomas Nelson, 1987).

Evelyn Eaton Whitehead and James D. Whitehead, *Marrying Well: Possibilities in Christian Marriage Today* (New York: Doubleday, 1981).

Philip Yancey, *After the Wedding* (Waco, Tex: Word, 1976).


**Magazines**

Marriage Partnership
Parents